Race, Remembering, and Jim Crow's Teachers

Studies in African American History and Culture

GRAHAM HODGES, *General Editor*

"White" Americans in "Black" Africa
Black and White American Methodist Missionaries in Liberia, 1820–1875
Eunjin Park

The Origins of the African American Civil Rights Movement, 1865–1956
Aimin Zhang

Religiosity, Cosmology, and Folklore
The African Influence in the Novels of Toni Morrison
Therese E. Higgins

Something Better for Our Children
Black Organizing in Chicago Public Schools, 1963–1971
Dionne Danns

Teach the Nation
Public School, Racial Uplift, and Women's Writing in the 1890s
Anne-Elizabeth Murdy

The Art of the Black Essay
From Meditation to Transcendence
Cheryl B. Butler

Emerging Afrikan Survivals
An Afrocentric Critical Theory
Kamau Kemayó

Slavery in the Cherokee Nation
The Keetoowah Society and the Defining of a People 1855–1867
Patrick N. Minges

Troubling Beginnings
Trans(per)forming African American History and Identity
Maurice E. Stevens

The Social Teachings of the Progressive National Baptist Convention, Inc., Since 1961
A Critical Analysis of the Least, the Lost, and the Left-out
Albert A. Avant, Jr.

Giving a Voice to the Voiceless
Four Pioneering Black Women Journalists
Jinx Coleman Broussard

Constructing Belonging
Class, Race, and Harlem's Professional Workers
Sabiyha Prince

Contesting the Terrain of the Ivory Tower
Spiritual Leadership of African-American Women in the Academy
Rochelle Garner

Post-Soul Black Cinema
Discontinuities, Innovations, and Breakpoints, 1970–1995
William R. Grant, IV

The Mysterious Voodoo Queen, Marie Laveaux
A Study of Powerful Female Leadership in Nineteenth-Century New Orleans
Ina Johanna Fandrich

Race and Masculinity in Contemporary American Prison Narratives
Auli Ek

Swinging the Vernacular
Jazz and African American Modernist Literature
Michael Borshuk

Boys, Boyz, Bois
An Ethics of Black Masculinity in Film and Popular Media
Keith M. Harris

Movement Matters
American Antiapartheid Activism and the Rise of Multicultural Politics
David L. Hostetter

Slavery, Southern Culture, and Education in Little Dixie, Missouri, 1820–1860
Jeffrey C. Stone

Courting Communities
Black Female Nationalism and "Syncre-Nationalism" in the Nineteenth-Century North
Kathy L. Glass

The Selling of Civil Rights
The Student Nonviolent Coordinating Committee and the Use of Public Relations
Vanessa Murphree

Black Liberation in the Midwest
The Struggle in St. Louis, Missouri, 1964–1970
Kenneth S. Jolly

When to Stop the Cheering?
The Black Press, the Black Community, and the Integration of Professional Baseball
Brian Carroll

The Rise and Fall of the Garvey Movement in the Urban South, 1918–1942
Claudrena N. Harold

The Black Panthers in the Midwest
The Community Programs and Services of the Black Panther Party in Milwaukee, 1966–1977
Andrew Witt

Words and Songs of Bessie Smith, Billie Holiday, and Nina Simone
Sound Motion, Blues Spirit, and African Memory
Melanie E. Bratcher

Blaxploitation Films of the 1970s
Blackness and Genre
Novotny Lawrence

Womanism, Literature, and the Transformation of the Black Community, 1965–1980
Kalenda Eaton

Racial Discourse and Cosmopolitanism in Twentieth-Century African American Writing
Tania Friedel

Audience, Agency and Identity in Black Popular Culture
Shawan M. Worsley

The Postwar Struggle for Civil Rights
African Americans in San Francisco, 1945–1975
Paul T. Miller

Race, Remembering, and Jim Crow's Teachers
Hilton Kelly

Race, Remembering, and Jim Crow's Teachers

Hilton Kelly

Routledge
Taylor & Francis Group
New York   London

First published 2010
by Routledge
711 Third Avenue, New York, NY 10017

Simultaneously published in the UK
by Routledge
2 Park Square, Milton Park, Abingdon, Oxon OX14 4RN

Routledge is an imprint of the Taylor & Francis Group, an informa business

First issued in paperback in 2012

© 2010 Taylor & Francis

Typeset in Sabon by IBT Global.

All rights reserved. No part of this book may be reprinted or reproduced or utilised in any form or by any electronic, mechanical, or other means, now known or hereafter invented, including photocopying and recording, or in any information storage or retrieval system, without permission in writing from the publishers.

Trademark Notice: Product or corporate names may be trademarks or registered trademarks, and are used only for identification and explanation without intent to infringe.

Library of Congress Cataloging-in-Publication Data
Kelly, Hilton.
  Race, remembering, and Jim Crow's teachers / by Hilton Kelly.
    p. cm. — (Studies in African American history and culture)
  Includes bibliographical references and index.
  1. African American teachers—History. 2. African Americans—Education—History. 3. Discrimination in education—United States—History. 4. Segregation in education—United States—History. 5. Segregation in education—Law and legislation—United States—History. 6. Southern States—Race relations—History. 7 United States—Race relations—History. I. Title.
  LC2731.K45 2010
  371.10089'96073—dc22
                              2009044605

ISBN13: 978-0-415-80478-3 (hbk)
ISBN13: 978-0-203-85235-4 (ebk)
ISBN13: 978-0-415-63804-3 (pbk)

In memory of my mother
Vernice Hyman Kelly Lindsey
and for
Jim Crow's teachers

Contents

Foreword   xiii
Acknowledgements   xvii

PART I
Remembering Teachers and Teaching

1   "Dying with One's Boots On": Collective Remembering of Legally Segregated Schools for Blacks and Its Teachers   3

2   You Must Remember This: Reconstructions of the Geopolitics of Race and Racism in the Jim Crow South   16

3   Voices of Collective Remembering: Black Teachers in Edgecombe, Nash and Wilson Counties   25

PART II
Hidden Transcripts Revealed

4   "The Way We Found Them to Be": Black Teachers and the Politics of Respectability in Jim Crow North Carolina   43

5   A Strategy of Opportunity: Black Teachers and the Making of a New Form of Capital   66

PART III
Remembering Jim Crow's Teachers

6   "The Half Had Not Been Told": Hidden Transcripts Made Public   93

Appendix A: Methodology	103
Appendix B: Interview questions	109
Appendix C: Table: Demographics and Characteristics of Participants	111
Notes	115
Bibliography	121
Index	129

The writing of history reflects the interests, predilections, and even prejudices of a given generation. This means that at the present time there is an urgent need to re-examine our past in terms of our present outlook.

The late John Hope Franklin,
African-American Biography, Vol. 2

In the hands of the Negro teachers rests the destiny of the race.

The late Ambrose Caliver,
Journal of Negro Education, 1935

Foreword

Oral history has served as a corrective to the accounts that are sponsored by those in dominant positions in society. There are those who still discount oral history as anecdotal and all too dependent on faulty memories. Both of course can be true but when critics see archival history as more objective I counter that archives only have the advantage of being recorded for reasons of their own. Archival history recounts the story of those who make the records—with all their vested interests and suppressed stories. My argument is that there is no reasonable claim to one or the other being a better method. History is better understood as a set of stories told and untold that we use to orient ourselves to the world about us. We cannot make a claim to objective accounts for history is fully constructed in social lives—both of those studied and those studying them. History is one way we make sense of the world. Its value is not in its abstraction from social life but from its injection into social life.

This is probably no more evident than in the study of race in the United States. It is not an accident that people of color have turned to oral history as a means to gain voice. The official story is literally a whitewash of experience. It is not only a story from the point of view of Whites—it is also written over the stories of people of color. Color and indeed variety are obliterated in the process. By valorizing the stories of everyday people, oral history has become a way to reveal the accounts suppressed both by White supremacy and the norms of academic scholarship. Through oral history, African Americans have given themselves a voice that had been denied them by speaking of the lives they have lived. What is inspiring is that these stories are not only accounts of the White racism that so shapes their lives. These oral histories are so much more—accounts of struggle, of perseverance, of invention and creativity, of the power of their humanity. Such histories have obviously much to teach our nation, if we are willing to learn.

Yet there is little evidence that Whites are willing to learn from those they see as the other. Whites, like me, have constructed our dominance in part through by establishing our forms of knowledge as the 'right' knowledge and thus others should learn from us—not the other way around. Thus as African Americans and others have found stories that have much to teach, it is not apparent that Whites will learn from these works. This is disastrous for the wider nation but is nowhere more devastating than in education. The current policy flap over the so-called achievement gap is a key case in point. The gap names African Americans as those who are not learning—rather than being seen as an artifact of Whites not learning from history. The question should not be how to make African American children learn more but rather how Whites destroyed African American academic achievement.

This question forces us back into history. We can point to the policies against educating African American slaves in the 1830s. We can point to race riots by Whites that largely disenfranchised African Americans during Reconstruction. We can point to the White created Jim Crow, segregated society. And we can point to school desegregation which in ending segregated schooling for a period of time also destroyed the Black middle class of teachers and made Black students more subject to White control of their learning. School desegregation ended the linkage between education, morality and emancipation in African American communities that Hilton Kelly shows so dramatically in this book. Kelly shows that while African Americans were being suppressed by segregated education in many ways, they were also using segregated education to create educational capital. School desegregation ended this capability because it was based on racist assumptions that Black teachers, schools and students were academically inferior. While Kelly is appropriately reluctant to draw policy directives for today from his work, I want to be clear that Black achievement was destroyed through measures like school desegregation and we will need more than an emphasis on testing and standards to reestablish it. I believe it will take something of the scale of school desegregation to deal with the achievement gap but I see no evidence that this is even being considered as necessary. This necessarily massive project will involve the mobilization of the African American community and directly address the assumptions of White superiority.

Segregation was, of course, morally abhorrent, and Kelly's work is not a justification of segregation. Rather he speaks of, and for, the capability of Black educators to use an under-resourced institution to make education possible, valued and productive. In this, we can learn that there is something about racial consciousness (or double consciousness) that is essential to learning. Yet in my own work in schools, speaking race is all too often viewed as dangerous. Given the research that shows that racial identity (including an awareness of racism that is motivating) is central to academic achievement of students of color, this suppression of race talk actively works against Black student achievement. Kelly shows that teachers in segregated Black schools gave race meaning. Black students, teachers and parents were united in their struggles against White dominance. In Kelly's view, this meaning became ensconced in hidden transcripts—hidden from Whites but widely shared across the Black community. In these transcripts, being Black was affirmed and racism was used to develop uniquely talented Black youth.

Again some may want to argue that this study as with any oral history study (Kelly uses archival sources as well it should be noted) is too anecdotal to be trusted. Yet Kelly is clear that this study is part of a set of studies that reveal common patterns. I call these studies the "what was lost" ethnohistories. These studies are remarkably similar in what they find was present in segregated education that was lost under desegregation. Many of these studies have been done in North Carolina and it may be that there is a state specific set of findings here. However, Kelly cites studies in other states as well. Thus I would argue that there is reason to believe that this study speaks to more general patterns that are worthy of our attention. Further, this set of studies also points to a characteristic of qualitative studies that is not emphasized enough. Quantitative studies work to accumulate a body of evidence that purportedly specifies the objective case. Qualitative studies, on the other hand, have a more discursive theory of truth. The goal of qualitative research is to enrich and enlarge the human discourse. Studies such as Kelly's and the other "what was lost" ethnohistories give us new understandings that lead us to think, speak and act in different ways if the studies are successful. As I said above, I am less than convinced that the White society is willing to engage this discourse as yet, but Kelly's book presents another articulation of this discourse. What Kelly adds to the discourse of the other studies is more than an understanding of the case in three counties in North Carolina. Kelly has engaged key theoretical constructs as well in his focus on hidden transcripts, educational capital, and double consciousness. With each of these (and others as well), Kelly advances a novel interpretation based on the particulars of his study. He uses theory to explain but also moves the theories he uses in new directions. The other "what was lost" ethnohistories tend to be more documentary than theoretical. This book shows that ethnohistories can both use and advance social theory in ways rarely attempted. He advances the scholarship in this area and speaks to broader theoretical interests at the same time. This pushes the discourse into new domains and hopefully will lead to others engaging what has been found here.

Studies of segregation continue to reveal the capability and resiliency of African Americans. Hilton Kelly has built upon the existing research in productive ways. He shows us how Black educators worked to promote high achievement and educational capital in their students. In doing so he uses theory in ways that both help explicate the data and show how these theories need adapting to be more useful in the study of race. This book changes how studies of segregation will be done from now forward. We all have much to learn here.

George W. Noblit
Joseph R. Neikirk Professor of Sociology of Education
University of North Carolina at Chapel Hill

Acknowledgements

Race, Remembering, and Jim Crow's Teachers has evolved over five years, from "a bit of a hunch" to a dissertation to this book. While I have Dan Clawson, Eleanor Townsley and John Bracey to thank for guiding me through an intellectual puzzle that I have tried to answer with rigor and with care, any errors or problems are mine alone. I could not have had a more thoughtful and hardworking graduate advisor than Dan Clawson. He shaped my ideas and my writing tremendously. Dan showed great excitement for the project from the very beginning and became my writing coach as I struggled to tell this nuanced and complicated story.

In addition to Dan, the initial project benefited from the sociological insights of Eleanor Townsley, a compassionate mentor and a critical reader of my work. We enjoyed numerous intense meetings at the Thirsty Mind Coffee Shop in South Hadley, Massachusetts, discussing the sociology profession, sociological theory (especially capital, field and habitus), and the micropolitics of getting a Ph.D. Long before my graduate work, however, John Bracey had been one of many scholars in the field of African-American Studies that I most admired. "Bracey" read my work at a moment in graduate school in which I had used up all the psychological tools and intellectual strategies that I had acquired as an undergraduate to navigate race and racism. Just in the nick of time, after a "drop by the office" conversation with him, I had a renewed sense of my abilities and "a plan." I remain very much in awe of his personal knowledge of African-American history and culture, and I am thankful for his willingness to share some of this knowledge with me.

I am grateful to the following former teachers of legally segregated schools for blacks and long-time members of Nash, Edgecombe, and Wilson counties in North Carolina who agreed to take part in the study: Annie Beasley, Alton Bobbitt, Charles Branford, Susie Branford, Maureen Brown, James Buchanan, Gloria Burks, Amanda Cameron, Carol Cooper, Fannie Coston, Elmer Cummings, Henry Davis, Josephine Edwards, the late Lucille Edwards, Athalene Emory, Thelma Forbes, Julia Foster, Terrence Foster, the late Gloria Gray, Samuel Gray, Arcenia Hines, Catherine Hines, Mildred Hines, Nellie Hunter, Doretha Jones, Jessie Jones, Cleveland Lewis,

Hazel Lewis, Equiller Lucas, Mary Odom, Roosevelt Pitt, Ada Pulley, Herbert Pulley, Joseph Ray, Anniebelle Ricks, Joseph Ricks, Effie Smith, Catherine Taylor, Helen Toney, Dianne Turner, William Turner, Vera Tyson, Pauline White, and James Williams.

My deepest regret is that my mother, Vernice Hyman Kelly Lindsey, did not live to see the book in print. My mother had been one of the greatest supporters of my intellectual pursuits. Her early emotional and financial support of my academic interests can probably best explain how a poor black boy from Sharpsburg, North Carolina earned a Ph.D. When I turned my bedroom into a classroom—chalk, bulletin board, and teaching manuals—my mother allowed me this space to explore and to dream even when she may have thought that I should have been out playing with other kids. She supplied me with a desk and a typewriter for Christmas when I could not have been more than nine or ten years old, simply because I wanted them. She paid for piano lessons when music became my "new thing," sent me to academic camps during the summers when science and math became my "new thing" and encouraged me to go to France when French became my "new thing." As a single-parent, she financed my education from kindergarten to graduate school. I miss my mother madly.

Both my maternal grandmother, the late Clara Mae Hyman Rand, and my paternal grandmother, the late Thelma Gray Kelly Lovely, deserve special mention as my earliest teachers and greatest emotional supporters. I am grateful also to my aunt, Clara Louise Knight, and my stepfather, Henry Lindsey, for helping me derive lists of teachers in Nash, Edgecombe, and Wilson counties who could potentially participate in my study. I am also greatly indebted to Portia Kelly Williams, my dear sister, Timothy Williams, my nephew, and Tim Williams, my brother-in-law. I have received a great deal of love and support from my sister, Portia, who was my sounding board in some of the worst moments in my life, my cheerleader at some of the highest points in my life, and my financier whenever the money was low (and it was always low). Tim has been very supportive as the first person I could call when I needed to move—again.

C. Shawn McGuffey and Luis Rivera have been my best friends since my graduate school days at the University of Massachusetts at Amherst. Kameeleon Johnson has been my best friend since college days at the University of North Carolina at Charlotte. Patricia Warren, LaVada Taylor Brandon, Theodorea Berry, Pilar Schiavo, April White, Nina Ha, Lucy Mae San Pablo Burns, Chanti Chantavong and Takiema Bunche-Smith have all thrown out life-lines and laughter at critical points in my life.

The book has been written because of financial support from three institutions. I have received several fellowships from the University of Massachusetts at Amherst throughout my graduate school career. I am most thankful for the University Fellowship which afforded me the opportunity to collect data in North Carolina and to pay for transcriptions. I also received the Consortium for Faculty Diversity (CFD) Dissertation Fellowship which allowed me to complete my dissertation at Denison University. That financial support and Denison's incredible resources enabled me to complete the dissertation in record time with little worries about money, resources and time. I am thankful for the colleagueship that I received at Denison University, especially from Anita Waters, Susan Diduk, Mary Tuominen, Kent Maynard, Kate O'Neil, VeVe LeLe, Bahram Tavokolian, John Jackson, Toni King, Donna Ellis, Niambi Carter, Lauren Araiza, Anita Mannur, Amy Scott-Douglass, Lisa Scott, Vincent Briley, Sue Davis, Jeremy Blake and Lynette Byrd.

At Davidson College, I revised every chapter of the dissertation and completed more research through a generous Faculty Study and Research Grant. I have been blessed with supportive colleagues: Carol Higham, Kristi Multhaup, Nancy Fairley, Brenda Flanagan, Sophia Sarafova, Karmella Haynes, Maria Fackler, Caroline Beschea-Fache, Fuji Lozada, Helen Cho, Gayle Kaufman, Gerardo Marti, Rick Gay, Barbara Lom, Scott Denham, Anne Blue Wills, Leslie Marsicano and Ann Douglass. Words simply cannot express the joy and excitement that I have gained from students who have shown interest in the book and have had some part to play in the final version of it: Whitney White, Darrell Scott, Carrie Boyle, Paul Bennett, Jordan Starck and Krystalin Bush.

Ultimately, *Race, Remembering, and Jim Crow's Teachers* would not have been possible without the published work of scholars writing on black teachers' lives and work. Although the list is much too long to provide each person's name here, I must mention the joy that I felt when I first discovered Linda Perkin's research on the history of blacks in teaching. Until then, it had not occurred to me that anyone else cared about the lives and work of black teachers. Perkins's work and area of interest led me to monographs, articles, and book chapters of James Anderson, Vanessa Siddle Walker, V.P. Franklin, Michele Foster, Michael Fultz, Adah Ward Randolph, George Noblit, Adam Fairclough, Heather Williams, Jeannine Dingus-Eason and many, many more. In addition, I have benefited from a wonderful association with brilliant colleagues and conference friends through the American Educational Studies Association: LaVada Taylor Brandon, Denise Taliaferro Baszile, Theodorea Berry, Sherick Hughes, Gloria Gibson, and Kristen Luschen.

In the end, this book is for Jim Crow's teachers who dedicated their lives to teaching in spite of everything.

Part I

Remembering Teachers and Teaching

1 "Dying with One's Boots On"
Collective Remembering of Legally Segregated Schools for Blacks and Its Teachers

In the summer of 1974, eleven former students of the Frederick Douglass School, a former all-black public school in Wilson County, North Carolina, founded an alumni association to commemorate the legacy of their alma mater which closed in 1969. As they gathered class pictures, started local and state chapters, and planned the first national alumni association meeting, the founding officers also drafted a biographical sketch of the school's first teacher and principal, Robert A. Johnson, who served from 1936–1966. After briefly mentioning his educational background, which included a master's degree in administration from New York University, the biography read:

> He was not just the principal of [Frederick Douglass] school; his services included teaching academic subjects and administering the details that accompany an effective high school program.... As further testimony to Mr. Johnson's dedication and interest in education, he traveled the back roads throughout Wilson County in his automobile to insure that children of high school eligibility were enrolled in school. The life and death of Mr. Johnson prompted the quotation ... 'dying with one's boots on' as indicative of one's dedication to hard work ... (*Frederick Douglass Alumni Association Souvenir Journal*, 1993)

The biography concluded with a ceremonious reminder of Principal Johnson's sudden death in his office just before the start of the school day on March 14, 1966. This particular impression suggests that black teachers and administrators were actively engaged in their work before and during the federal mandate to desegregate public schools in the South (See also, Perkins, 1989; Cecelski, 1994; Siddle Walker, 1996; Fairclough, 2001, 2007; Ramsey, 2008).

The image of Jim Crow's teachers—former teachers who taught in legally segregated schools for blacks—being engaged in hard work at the point of death addresses one of the most important and the most disputed topics in educational discourse.[1] As part of a collective memory of Frederick Douglass School, the narrative of Principal Johnson dying with his boots on challenges dominant narratives of poorly trained black teachers and self-serving black middle class professionals (Bond, 1934; Frazier, 1957; Tyack and Cuban, 1995; Patterson, 2001).[2] "The narrative of one life is part of an interconnecting set of narratives; it is embedded in the story of those groups from which individuals derive their identity," as Paul Connerton (1989, p. 21) pointed out. Commemorations, such as the annual gathering of the Frederick Douglas Alumni Association, provide an occasion for the public reconstruction of what legally segregated schools for blacks used to be from the memories of former students, teachers, and community members.

Race, Remembering, & Jim Crow's Teachers examines both "how" and "what" teachers—who were also students of all-black public high schools—remember about the quality and character of teachers and teaching. I argue that teachers were a major resource for black achievement and social mobility; they fashioned situated pedagogies for the acquisition of skills, knowledge, and credentials that could be used in exchange for jobs, civil rights, and social power. However, the argument demands reconsideration of the social and geopolitical context in which black teachers worked and clarification of the attitudes, beliefs, and motivations that they held. It also requires searching for and mining out "hidden transcripts," or latent oral and written reports of the social world created in the all-black school, that is not a part of the public record and memory of legally segregated schooling for blacks (Scott, 1990). Ultimately, the work of Jim Crow's teachers has the potential to inform contemporary discussions about educating today's African-American youth under power-laden circumstances, especially the continuing significance of inequity, racism, and resegregation in schooling (Dixson and Rousseau, 2006; Yosso, 2006; Taylor, Gillborn, & Ladson-Billings, 2009).

In an effort to understand the teacher's role in the social and historical foundations of black social mobility through formal schooling, this book addresses two enduring questions: 1.) What was the quality and character of teachers and teaching in legally segregated schools for blacks? 2.) In spite of state-sponsored racism and discrimination, how did teachers prepare black youth for skilled jobs, civil rights, and social power?

CONFLICT IN MEMORY: REMEMBERING FROM EXPERIENCE AND TEXTS

Within the contemporary United States, multiple collective memories of legally-segregated schools for blacks exist. On the one hand, there is a profoundly negative collective memory of black schools before integration as "inherently inferior" compared to their white counterparts. On the other hand, there is an overwhelmingly positive collective memory of the "remarkably good" all-black school among some former students, teachers, and community members in spite of white racism and discrimination.

Conflict in collective memories of the all-black public school presents an intellectual puzzle. The simplest explanation, according to James Wertsch (2002), is that a conflict in collective memories "[emerge] because members of a group all have participated in the event being remembered and hence have memories of it based on their individual experience" (p. 25). However, this explanation raises more questions than it answers: How do we explain memories that are not grounded in direct, immediate experience of events? How do we talk about a multigenerational sharing of a collective memory, or what Errante (2000) calls "vicarious memories?" Why does one collective memory dominate another, such as the memory of the all-black public school as inherently inferior over the memory of those same schools as remarkably good?

While members of a group do recall past events from their experiences, I contend that remembering is an active process in which how we remember is influenced by something other than individual experience. "Memory is not simply an exercise of recalling; there are many ways of remembering and different reasons why we may (or may not) want to remember," according to Errante (2000, p. 17). In *Voices of Collective Remembering*, James Wertsch (2002) introduced a more complex perspective of multiple or "multivoiced" collective memories attributable to texts, not only experience. According to Wertsch:

> Memory—both individual and collective—is viewed as 'distributed' between agent and texts, and the task becomes one of listening for the texts and the voices behind them as well as the voices of the particular individuals using these texts in particular settings. (p. 6)

From this perspective, there are several key points that must be highlighted: 1.) Individual and collective memory do not have to be grounded in or based upon experience; 2.) Individuals do not simply possess collective memory rather they draw upon it through different mediating texts to recall the past; and 3.) There are different and multivoiced collective memories because there are different assessments of the past.

Before I elaborate on these key points, I wish to explain briefly what I mean by "collective memory." In his pre-WWII pioneering work on collective memory, Maurice Halbwach argued that collective memory is essentially a social phenomenon in which individuals and groups reconstruct the past in light of the *present* (Coser, 1992; Olick & Robbins, 1998). More recently, scholars (Frentress and Wickham, 1992; Middleton and Edwards, 1990) have continued to argue that collective memory is greatly influenced by the *present*. While I agree with the basic tenet of this tradition in collective memory studies that the present shapes memories of the past, the emphasis in this book is focused on how oral and written texts mediate remembering and reconstructions of the past. The task before me and others, then, is less about identifying "the present in memories of the past" but more about recognizing the texts that support a particular collective memory (For example, Liberato, Fennell, & Jeffries, 2008). Individuals and groups possess different images and different texts from the past which structures their feelings about the present social order.

Returning to the key points in Wertsch's theory of collective remembering, the first stated that individual and collective memory can be mediated through texts. In other words, individuals and groups can recall past events by drawing upon oral and written texts that shape how they remember the past. Multivoiced collective memories are the result of multiple narrative texts produced by the individual, the group, the state, and the media, which are "consumed, or used, by individuals and groups" (Wertsch, 2002, p. 6). Individuals are members of a textual community as much as they are members of a cultural group which has implications for remembering.[3] As Wertsch explained: "Some members of a textual community may not have even read the text, but by participating in the activities of a textual community, they can have the access to the textual material around which the group is organized" (p. 28). Therefore, it is not just individuals who experience an event who can recall it; individuals who may not have been alive to experience an event may recall it through textual communities.

The second key point stated that individuals do not simply possess collective memory rather they draw upon it. "Remembering is a form of mediated action," as Wertsch (2002) argued, "which entails the involvement of active agents and cultural tools" (p. 13). If we want to understand how people remember, we have to listen for the texts and the voices that mediate a collective memory. What are the texts that support narratives of the "inferior" all-black school? What are the texts that support narratives of the "good" all-black school? Who are the voices behind each of these narratives? While multiple generations can draw upon the same texts to remember the past, conflicts in memory can occur when different groups draw upon different texts. Moreover, as Jan Assmann (1995) stated:

> Every individual memory constitutes itself in communication with others. These 'others,' however, are not just any set of people, rather they are groups who conceive their unity and peculiarity through a common image of their past . . . Every individual belongs to numerous such groups and therefore entertains numerous collective self-images and memories. (127)

Like Wertsch, Assmann also discussed remembering as an active process that is drawn upon by individuals in groups.

The third key point stated that there are different and multivoiced collective memories because there are different assessments of the past. For example, in *The Dream Long Deferred*—a paper about the integration of the Charlotte-Mecklenburg School System in North Carolina—Frye Gaillard (1988) pointed out that different assessments of events during the tumultuous early integration years shaped the way that blacks and whites remembered those same events. Gaillard wrote, convincingly:

> Members of the white community, particularly the business and political leadership, had tended to be proud of the city's racial progress. They spoke enthusiastically about voluntary gestures toward the goal of integration—the removal of racial barriers in downtown restaurants, or the successful experiment at Central High School, where Gus Roberts broke the color line in 1957.... But in the black community, the view was different. There, leaders tended to emphasize the ordeal of Dorothy Counts, who, also in 1957, was driven out of Harding High [School] by petty acts of violence and the threat of something worse. They would mention the bombing of the homes of civil rights leaders, and they would point out that political and economic power was almost entirely in the hands of whites. (p. 184)

By listening for the texts and the particular voices of individuals, it is possible to uncover which texts are being consumed and which texts are being neglected or overlooked (Wertsch, 2002).

In the end, all texts are not equal, public and available. In the account above, Gaillard directs our attention to the power-laden situation in which many texts have been written or heard. Some texts are public, for example, while others are hidden. Some texts remain hidden for decades (and even centuries) until power changes, lying dormant until they can be revealed with little to no retribution. Some texts are never made available for individuals to draw upon, while others are made official and certified as "truth." Keeping in mind the conflict in memory over legally segregated schools for blacks and its teachers, one possible way to solve this intellectual puzzle is through a consideration of the texts that groups draw upon to remember. While collective memories can be based on individual and group experiences, I argue that collective memories also "share a representation of the past because they share textual resources" (Wertsch, 2002, p. 26).

STATE PRODUCTION OF OFFICIAL MEMORY: THE "INFERIOR" ALL-BLACK SCHOOL

My first encounter with a negative collective memory of legally segregated schools for blacks occurred in a college classroom. In a seminar on the schooling of African-Americans in the United States, I asked students probing questions about the kind of education that blacks received before the 1954 *Brown* decision. Having been aware that students were recently inundated with the history and logic of the *Brown* decision at its 50th anniversary, I wondered whether or not students had learned anything different from what they had been taught in elementary and high school. Quite the opposite of what I expected happened, students *still* talked about the lack of resources, the unequal facilities, and the poor academic standards *as if they had lived through it themselves.* Students' vicarious memories of the all-black school before desegregation had a particular focus on resource deprivation and educational barriers such that the only way blacks could have received a good education was through the dismantling of *their* schools.[4] But could these assumptions and sentiments be linked to particular texts that students might have read or heard throughout their K-12 schooling experiences?

Thinking back to students' recollections of the inferior all-black school, I searched for texts that may have mediated such a profoundly negative collective memory. The most obvious texts have been the 1954 and 1955 *Brown v. Board of Education, Topeka, Kansas* Supreme Court decisions (Martin, 1998). Through textual mediation, such as print journalism, television, textbooks, and word-of-mouth, my students (and I) have been influenced by a particular collective memory of "Jim Crow schooling." More specifically, this collective memory has produced one single assessment of "inferior" all-black schools with negative assumptions about the intellectual capabilities of both black students and teachers in those schools. In the unanimous 1954 *Brown* decision, for example, part of the majority opinion read:

> Segregation of white and colored children in public schools has a detrimental effect upon the colored children. The impact is greater when it has the sanction of the law; for the policy of separating the races is usually interpreted as denoting the inferiority of the Negro group. A sense of inferiority affects the motivation of the child to learn. Segregation with the sanction of law, therefore, has a tendency to [retard] the educational and mental development of Negro children and to deprive them of some of the benefits they would receive in a racial[ly] integrated system. (Mullane, 1993, p. 629)

As I have stated, the stories that my students recalled and retold in my classroom have been shaped by the wording and sentiments of the 1954 *Brown* decision, a historical and cultural text. While there are other texts that have contributed to the production of the official collective memory of legally segregated schools for blacks, I emphasize the 1954 *Brown* decision for its far-reaching and deliberate attempt to frame the need for school desegregation.

Through the authority and prestige of the United States Supreme Court, students learned—many years after the fact—that "a sense of inferiority affects the motivation of the [black] child to learn." Looking back at the quotation above, notice that the effects of segregation only harms the black child—not the white one. Moreover, students have been told (or have read) that "segregation," not white racism and discrimination, have "a tendency to [retard] the educational and mental development of Negro children" and "deprive them of some of the benefits" of a racially integrated school system.

When students and others draw upon this particular text to imagine what the all-black public school might have been, the danger involved is that it distorts the way these schools were to the people who attended them. Many decades later, my students drew upon textual resources that produced imagery of the damaged black psyche which has been made public and available in their state-adopted textbooks—a textual community (For a full discussion of the image of the damaged black psyche, see Scott, 1997).

Within the state production of a negative collective memory of legally segregated schools for blacks, the actions of white people are rarely identified as detrimental to the well-being of black youth in schools. Segregation has a damaging effect on black youth, not the decisions of white educational authorities and state-sponsored racial discrimination. In addition, the dominant narrative teaches that black children in segregated schools were mentally and psychologically damaged due to "inherently inferior" schools (Scott, 1997). Therefore, black youth would benefit—socially, intellectually, and culturally—from the mixing of white and black children in schools. Such (racial) thinking is implicit in the *Brown* decision and has had a major influence on the way our society remembers legally segregated schools for blacks.

THE PRODUCTION OF COUNTER-MEMORIES: THE "REMARKABLY GOOD" ALL-BLACK SCHOOL

As early as the mid-1960s and 1970s, there has been a conscious effort to produce counter-memories that challenge dominant perceptions, attitudes, and histories of legally segregated schools for blacks (Hundley, 1965; Perry, 1975; Sowell, 1976). More recently, a new cadre of scholars have continued to document and to reconstruct the good and valued all-black school (See Beauboeuf-Lafontant, 1999, 2002; Cecelski, 1994; Chafe, Gavins, & Korstad, 2001; Dougherty, 1998; Fairclough, 2000, 2001, 2004, 2007; Foster, 1990, 1991, 1993, 1997; Jeffries, 1994; Morris and Morris 2002; Noblit and Dempsey, 1996; Perkins 1989; Philipsen, 1993, 1999; Randolph, 2004; Shircliffe, 2006; Siddle Walker, 1996a, 1996b, 2000, 2001, 2005; White, 2004). Together, all of these texts forge a collective memory emphasizing overlooked and forgotten memories among former students, teachers, administrators, and community members. Unfortunately, only a small subset of the published literature looks specifically at teachers' lives and work systematically. There has not been enough effort to move beyond "experiences" toward a critical examination of oral history narratives as texts that challenge how our society remembers legally segregated schools for blacks.

Some of the common themes and characteristics of the literature on segregated schooling for blacks have been critically reviewed in an exhaustive study by educational historian Vanessa Siddle Walker (2000) titled, "Valued Segregated Schools for African American Children in the South, 1935-1969: A Review of Common Themes and Characteristics." Siddle Walker summarized the negative collective memory as follows: "The African-American segregated school is depicted as inferior because of inequality in facilities, lack of transportation, shorter school terms, teacher-pupil conflicts, overcrowding, poor teaching, and poor student attendance" (p. 253). In her effort to explain the "inescapable conclusion" that is interwoven into the tapestry of a dominant and official collective memory, Siddle-Walker pointed to "methodological dictates" and "limited knowledge and contact of many European American researchers with the [black] community" (p. 254). She concluded that it is these factors—methodology and contact—that can best explain the conflict in memory over the all-black school. Siddle Walker also referred to the overuse of the archives which is devoid of the voices and the perspectives of former students, teachers, and community members. In her work, Siddle Walker highlighted and celebrated the use of the "oral interview as a mode of historical inquiry" which can produce new narratives that support stories of inequality (p. 254).

This book, however, aims to reframe the discussion away from a critique of the historian's craft—its methodology and its contacts. I maintain that there is conflict in the memories themselves due to different assessments of the past mediated through texts. Most of the public texts have sought "to describe the segregated schools for their inequities and fail to include the themes and characteristics that were valued by the school community" as Siddle-Walker (2000, p. 278) noted. In her synthesis of the extant literature of segregated schools (including case studies and surveys) that make up nearly all the subordinated texts of the all-black public school in the South, Siddle Walker declared that:

> . . . the segregated schools in the South appear to have certain consistent characteristics. These include exemplary teachers and principals who increasingly were well trained and who created their own culture of teaching; curricular and extracurricular activities that reinforced the values of the school and the community; parental support of school, both in its financial needs and its cultural programs; and school principals who provided the leadership that implemented the vision that parents and teachers held about how to uplift the race. (p. 276)

All things considered, the production of a positive collective memory has created new story lines, uncovered entirely different plots, and revealed brand new actors. More importantly, hidden transcripts have revealed different assessments of the past that can no longer be ignored or overlooked.

ORAL INTERVIEWS AS TEXTS

There is a collective memory of the all-black public school that can be seen, heard, and felt at annual alumni celebrations that is multigenerational.

Beyond the notion that former students, teachers, and community members remember from their experiences, there has been little effort to understand these memories in any other way. Of special note and consideration, however, are scholars who dismiss these memories as nostalgia or romanticizing the past (Shircliffe, 2001; 2006). For example, Barbara Shircliffe (2001) writes:

> Former students' and teachers' romanticized memories of their school experience create an artful critique of the discriminatory aspects of the school desegregation process. . . . In their nostalgia for [black schools], however, former students and teachers are not claiming African Americans benefited from school segregation, but rather, they are pointing to the ironic legacy of desegregation and the tension between community control and integration. (p. 60)

Framing positive memories of legally segregated schooling as only nostalgia undermines the integrity of former students and teachers who have the capacity to remember their past as they lived it.

Despite the documented inequities between black and white schools before integration, I argue unequivocally that former teachers are actually saying that African Americans benefited from segregated schooling. The idea that there could have been no benefits in the all-black public school illustrates the limits of the dominant collective memory of these schools. Indeed, my analysis will uncover the ways in which students might have benefited from their teachers and their schools. If we are asked to consider that the personal and social memories of former black students, teachers, and parents are "romanticizing the past," then we should also wonder whether Shircliffe, and others, are not "romanticizing the present."

While a growing number of scholars have presented oral interview data in which "experience" or "nostalgia" has been used to frame collective remembering of the all-black school, I offer a different way of thinking about it through an analysis of oral interviews as texts. When oral interviews are considered as texts, scholars can begin to read these transcripts as something that could only be known from a particular positionality—on the other side of the tracks and behind the walls of segregation. In fact, I argue that the production of a subordinate collective memory has existed in oral form since the first schools were integrated; yet, we have not thought about them as texts that individuals draw upon to remember. Some of these texts are written narratives that can be found in archives, while others exist only as vicarious memories passed down within families and among former students, teachers, and community members themselves (Fabre & O'Meally, 1994; Foster, 1997).

But there are at least two reasons why an overwhelmingly positive collective memory about segregated schools has come under attack for being nostalgic. First, researchers have allowed the constant comparison between segregated schools and integrated schools in their interviews. Like most informants or interviewees who are asked to remember historical events, black teachers who are asked about the past in the present tend to talk about the "golden years" or "paradise lost" in an unstructured interview (White, 2004). In oral history interviewing, the focus must be on what it was like to teach in all-black schools **before integration**, making every effort to move teachers away from constant comparisons of "before" and "after" integration.

Second, the geographically scattered nature of most of this research makes any good memories seem isolated, personal, and anecdotal. Researchers should seek to locate a network of teachers who live in close proximity, but did not necessarily teach in the same school in order to establish emergent patterns and core experiences. In addition, scholars must work to build upon scholarship in the same geographic region to complicate what we know and to present more nuanced arguments and perspectives (See Siddle Walker, 1996b; Cecelski, 1994; Philipsen, 1993, 1999; Chafe, Gavins & Korstad, 2001). Otherwise, much of this research will seem disconnected and anecdotal, even when scholars have been quite systematic and careful.

Scholars differ in their assessment of the credibility and truthfulness of oral interviews many years after the fact. For example, as I mentioned earlier, some scholars have dismissed good memories of "segregated schooling" as simply romanticizing the past, while others view the evidence as anecdotal with problems in methodology and personal bias (Dougherty, 1999). While I never accepted "nostalgia" as the only way to understand the conflict in memory over legally segregated schools for blacks, I did assume originally that the issue was simply a matter of color—blacks remembering one way and whites remembering another way. Research, however, has shown that there are multiple variables to be considered in how people remember, such as age, place, and space (Kruger-Kahloula, 1994; Schwartz and Schuman, 2005; Tickamyer, 2000). Moreover, different generations remember different things (Schuman and Scott, 1989). People in one place (e.g., on the west coast) might remember something different from people in another place (e.g., on the east coast) depending upon the saliency of the experience. While all these variables make sense, we often do not think about how individual and collective remembering can be textually-mediated such that who remembers does not matter as much as the texts that they draw upon to remember.

HIDDEN TRANSCRIPTS IN MEMORIES OF LEGALLY SEGREGATED SCHOOLS FOR BLACKS

How, then, can we understand the different texts and voices of collective remembering? I have made the case that the dominant voice in the telling and retelling of the history and memory of legally segregated schools for blacks derives from a textual community, emphasizing that they were "inherently inferior" in newspaper articles, television shows, history textbooks and documentaries. The well-known example is the 1954 *Brown* decision, which certainly contributed to the dominant collective memory. For the most part, the public message has been that segregated schooling for blacks was a failure and that integrated schooling has been a great success. At the 50th anniversary of *Brown*, however, the counter-memories of former teachers, students, and community members served as hidden texts in many conference presentations and campus events that I attended. While it is no longer socially acceptable to talk about the all-black school before integration as a complete failure, still there are some who are just not willing to accept that these schools might have been remarkably good. After all, some might argue, these schools lacked resources and funding that would have made it difficult for them to function effectively. Perhaps, only half of the story has been told. It continues to be important, then, to document and to analyze different voices of collective remembering so that we understand why there might be good memories—right along with the bad.

A positive collective memory of legally segregated schools for blacks and its teachers can be understood more completely through the unveiling of hidden transcripts—latent oral and written reports of the social world created and lived in the all-black school before integration (Scott, 1990). In the late 1970s, for example, Sowell (1976) published an article entitled, *Patterns of Black Excellence*, in which he basically asked the question: If segregated schools for blacks were so terrible, why are there patterns of black excellence throughout the United States in the Age of Jim Crow? He provided a long list of well-known and successful blacks in American life and culture as convincing evidence that there must have been some "good" in all-black public schools. The most ironic example might be the late Supreme Court Justice Thurgood Marshall who attended all-black public schools from grades 1–12 and later attended a historically black university and law school. It was through Marshall's leadership, brilliance, and perseverance that we have a 1954 *Brown* decision at all (Williams, 1998). This book calls attention to the need to re-conceptualize oral interviews as hidden transcripts created and remembered from the past, not the present. In addition, the book presents a multi-site study which seeks to look into classrooms and schools (that no longer exist) in order to uncover the hidden transcripts that former teachers draw upon to remember.

There are many reasons why we should record and study the memories of former teachers. First, the population is declining due to old age, sickness, and memory loss. Second, black teachers—in particular—were uniquely located within the larger Jim Crow society as members of the black middle class within a closed opportunity structure in the U.S. Despite their high position and status in black society, black teachers had to negotiate and navigate their social positions in two worlds—black and white. Third, which is also related to the second reason, there is still little agreement about the degree to which black teachers promoted the status quo or promoted civil rights in their fight for "respectability" in both the North and South. (Respectability commonly refers to efforts among middle class professional blacks who actively sought to prove to whites that blacks possessed high morals, high culture, and high intelligence.) As historian David Cecelski (1994) reminded us, and it remains true today, "no commemorative markers reveal what the black schools used to be, who once studied and taught in them, or why so many closed their doors a generation ago. Behind their weathered facades and boarded-up windows lies an important, hidden chapter in American history" (p. 7).

OVERVIEW OF THE BOOK

After making presentations on black teachers' memories about segregated schools to academic audiences at conferences in 2004 and 2005, I noticed that different people kept asking the same questions in different ways: "If black schools were so good, then why did blacks want to integrate?" Like Vanessa Siddle Walker, Barbara Shircliffe, Adah Ward Randolph and others, who probably answered a similar question on all-black schools in the South, the Panhandle and the North, respectively, I felt compelled to provide a thoughtful response to at least the first part of the question, reformulated as: how can we explain good memories of segregated schools for blacks? This book is my answer but also it is my effort to introduce a new theoretical framework to understand the (re)emergence of stories and histories of the good all-black school, in particular, and the undeniable conflict in collective memories, in general.

I have divided *Race, Remembering, and Jim Crow's Teachers* into three parts. The first part consists of three chapters that provide both an introduction and the context for understanding why former teachers might have remarkably good memories of their segregated schools. Chapters II and III examine the geopolitics of race and racism in Jim Crow North Carolina from the perspectives and collective remembering of former teachers. Their memories challenge some negative images and unknown (or forgotten) meanings of living and learning in the Jim Crow South. Drawing upon participants' reconstructions of the past and their voices of collective remembering, chapters II and III will uncover the hidden world that blacks created behind "the walls of segregation," to borrow a phrase used by sociologist E. Franklin Frazier (1957). More importantly, former teachers will establish their roles within black communities and reveal how they worked to prepare black youth for a world that simply did not exist—free and open to black talent and ambition.

The second part of the book stands alone as two counter-narratives to a dominant collective memory of "inherently inferior" teachers and teaching in the all-black school. Given that former teachers remember from hidden transcripts, Chapters IV and V lay out and interrogate "what" they remember. More specifically, Chapter IV reconsiders the political nature of a respectability discourse among participants. Writing against images of materialistic and status-addicted black middle class teachers, I argue that the politics of respectability shaped teachers' perceptions and actions in positive ways. Instead of limiting or constraining black teachers' work, the politics of respectability actually gave them a sense of purpose and hope to forge ahead.

Chapter V introduces "educational capital" as a new concept to explain how former teachers of legally-segregated schools for blacks prepared and motivated disadvantaged students in spite of unequal funding and resource deprivation. Black teachers fashioned situated pedagogies for the acquisition of skills, knowledge, and credentials that could be used in exchange for jobs, rights, and social power. I outline four strategies of opportunity which provide clues to how teachers today can educate poor children of color with little resources in the age of resegregated schools: 1.) Generating materials and supplies, 2.) Situating curriculum and instruction, 3.) Mobilizing human resources and 4.) Forging double consciousness among students.

Chapter VI concludes the book with an evaluation of participants' beliefs and actions as read and interpreted from their oral narratives. After reviewing the main argument and major discussions presented, I explain that the purpose of the book is *not* to make suggestions for the preparation of teachers or to prescribe best teaching practices. Understanding the different world and circumstances in which Jim Crow's teachers worked, I offer foundational principles that are useful and necessary to live by as we continue to educate disadvantaged youth with paltry resources and unequal funding in resegregated schools.

2 You Must Remember This
Reconstructions of the Geopolitics of Race and Racism in the Jim Crow South

In the late 1920s, Josephine Edwards attended a graded school in rural Nash County, North Carolina, with a pot-belly stove in the middle of the classroom, an outdoor toilet for the teacher and the students, and hand-me-down books that parents had purchased originally for older siblings at a local store. Under these conditions, Edwards graduated from an all-black two-teacher school in the seventh grade and later graduated from the high school department of the Nash Central Training School for Negroes. In a graded school, according to educational historian James Leloudis (1996), "teachers measured children's success and made promotions from one grade level to the next on the basis of an ability to perform according to uniform criteria. Advancement was to be earned, not awarded on the basis of family, friendship, patronage, or some other particularistic relation" (p. 23). These milestones were remarkable when you consider that it had only been "in 1914 that the first three public black high schools in North Carolina were opened, and in 1919 the first black high schools were accredited, four public and seven private" (Rodgers, 1975, p. 30).

In an interview, Edwards recalled: "We had to pass an achievement test before we were allowed to enter high school. And high school, when I went, started in the 8th grade."

Kelly: What was the last grade required to complete high school?
Edwards: 11th grade. High schools were 8th through 11th grade. I can recall in high school my freshman year, we had general science, and English, and general math. The books were hand-me-down and forgive me if I [digress] a little because I am going back. My mother had to buy our books when we were down in the lower grades. I had a brother older than I and the books were hand-me-downs, but some of them weren't. Later, the state furnished books. The whites got the new editions ... and when they got new editions, we got their old editions.
Kelly: Can you say more about this?
Edwards: I remember how we would be reading a story and you would turn the page and the next page was gone. You had to surmise

what the story was like. . . . I taught out of the same reader that I studied when I was in the 5th grade. I saw some of the children's names in books that I knew when I grew up. [shaking] I get emotional when I think about it. How we forged, in spite of the atrocious things that were handed down to us and put on us.

These personal recollections are reconstructions of the past. More than an account of resource deprivation in the form of second-hand books and pot-belly stoves, Edwards and other participants in this study provide stories about how the geopolitics of race and racism shaped their schooling and teaching experiences in Jim Crow North Carolina. By geopolitics, I mean that geography (the location, size, and resources of a place) played a major role in the politics of race relations between blacks and whites (Delaney, 1998). In order to understand my analysis of the collective remembering among the participants I interviewed, it is necessary to lay out the social and geopolitical context in which these teachers acquired an education, became professionals, and "taught school." Edwards's comment that "the whites got the new editions . . . we [got] their old editions," for example, is located in a particular time (the Age of Jim Crow), place (the coastal plain of North Carolina), and space (the black community). In retrospect, many decades after the fact, Edwards reported that in spite of state-sponsored racial prejudice and discrimination, black people "forged."

Without knowing about the responses and the initiatives which characterized the work of Jim Crow's teachers, which Edwards talked about as "forging," these recollections could be easily dismissed as feelings of nostalgia. As I argued in Chapter 1, these accounts uncover hidden transcripts about teaching in legally segregated schools for blacks. In order to understand these reconstructions of the past, the geopolitical context and complexity which shaped black teachers' work must be remembered. In this chapter, I explore the social meanings of living in a legally segregated society through an analysis of Richard Wright's "The Ethics of Living Jim Crow." In the next chapter, I examine several emergent themes from participants' collective remembering as hidden transcripts that offer spatial clarity and give us a sense of the social organization of the all-black public high school and its teachers in North Carolina. In what follows, I draw upon literary, secondary historical and archival data to support my claims.

Black teachers used teaching as a geopolitical practice to change the spatial conditions in which blacks lived. In other words, they sought ways in which the next generation could cross the color line into white public space to access jobs, civil rights, and social power. As Delaney (1998) used the term, a "geopolitical practice" refers to "those social and political actions oriented toward reshaping the spatial conditions of social life . . . [including] such practices as firebombing, lynching, picketing, demonstrating, schooling, and preaching" (p. 10). A geopolitical practice has the potential for social domination and subordination when you consider the actions of whites, such as implementing segregation laws and restrictive housing covenants. I make the case that black teachers in my study engaged teaching as a geopolitical practice intended to prepare black youth for skilled jobs, civil rights, and social power. Thus, an impending question remains: How did teachers, like Edwards, forge in the face of state-sponsored racial prejudice and discrimination? Throughout the book, I address this query through the unveiling of hidden transcripts (stories, testimonies, and memories) from interviews with 44 former teachers who are long-term residents of black communities in Edgecombe, Nash and Wilson counties. Appendix A provides a detailed discussion of the methodology I used. (For a list of the questions that I asked and demographic data on participants, see appendices B and C.) Next, I explain what it meant to live as a black person in the Jim Crow South. I aim to push conventional thinking about the geopolitics of segregation beyond locating borders, identifying markers, and drawing lines toward really understanding the "social meanings" of living Jim Crow.

THE SOCIAL MEANINGS OF JIM CROW

In "Race, Place & the Law," David Delaney (1998) examined "the centrality of space, place, or geography in the historical constitution of race" (p. 3). Although he focused mainly on the early years of Jim Crow, Delaney's work has greatly influenced my thinking about the geopolitics of race and racism in segregated North Carolina. "It is hard to understate the central significance of geographical themes—space, place, and mobility—to the social and political history of race relations and antiblack racism in the United States," as Delaney (1998, p. 9) concluded. Furthermore, he writes, "segregation, integration, and separation are spatial processes . . . ghettos and exclusionary suburbs are spatial entities . . . access, exclusion, confinement, sanctuary, forced, or forcibly limited mobility are spatial experiences" (p. 9). In oral history interviewing, unless probing questions are asked, the geopolitical context and complexities are usually assumed by the interviewee; the social meanings of words, phrases, and sentiments are seldom articulated to the interviewer. Refer back to a snippet of the interview between Edwards and me in the introduction. Notice that I asked a fairly simple probing question (Can you say more about that?) to which the emotions attached to receiving "the old editions" took on new meanings and revealed hidden social relations between blacks and whites.

One of the most informative examples of "social meanings" is thoughtfully illustrated in Richard Wright's "The Ethics of Living Jim Crow: An Autobiographical Sketch," a literary and sociological masterpiece. The central character—whose name we are never given—recalls the very day, hour, and moment that he learned what it meant to be a black male on the colored side of the railroad tracks in rural Arkansas. I use rather lengthy segments from Wright's published work because I think it is important to see fully and to read completely the "geographical" and "spatial" language in which he chooses to describe the socialization process for blacks (and whites) in the Jim Crow South. Wright possessed an ease with articulating the impact of time, place, and space on black life and culture in his own reconstruction of the past. Wright's narrative underscores the centrality of the geopolitics of race and racism in the everyday lives of black people and bears out the often unarticulated meanings tied to living in a Jim Crow society.

What I hope this book will do that Wright's narrative never intended to do is to uncover what it meant to be a black teacher in the Age of Jim Crow. On the one hand, they had the responsibility to educate black youth for social mobility and racial uplift. On the other hand, they possessed enough education and liberal ideas to be considered a danger to the ruling white way of life. As later chapters move us into this direction, Wright's narrative takes us "behind the veil," in the Du Boisian sense, to explore the central character's first contact with white people, his first lessons in the rules of social interaction between blacks and whites and his efforts to find employment in white public space. Wright (1937/2001) began:

> *My first lesson in how to live as a Negro came when I was quite small. We were living in Arkansas. Our house stood behind the railroad tracks. Its skimpy yard was paved with black cinders. Nothing green ever grew in that yard. The only touch of green we could see was far away, beyond the tracks, over where the white folks lived. But cinders were good enough for me, and I never missed the green growing things.* (p. 21)

In the Age of Jim Crow, with very few exceptions, the inequalities between blacks and whites were visible. Blacks and whites in the South lived and died on different sides of the tracks or in different sections of town, with rules for social interaction or racial etiquette (Woodward, 1955/1974; Kruger-Kahloula, 1994). Whether they were wealthy educational leaders or poor tenant farmers, white people "stood firm in keeping blacks from sharing space in almost every enterprise in the Jim Crow years" (Franklin, 1994, p. 11). Delaney (1998) noted that whites also engaged in geopolitical practices, such as "evicting or denying access to housing in certain neighborhoods, posting Whites Only signs over doorways, ignoring such signs, passing statutes authorizing or mandating racial exclusions, and issuing judicial opinions and decrees validating or voiding these statutes" (p. 9). As historian David Cecelski (1994) concluded, "racial segregation stretched from the church to the graveyard, the schools to downtown businesses, social occasions to sports events" (p. 22). In practice, racial segregation meant that blacks would be relegated to the worst land areas or given restricted access to public accommodations. Wright (1937/2001) continued:

> *I never fully realized the appalling disadvantages of a cinder environment till one day the gang to which I belonged found itself engaged in a*

> *war with the white boys who lived beyond the tracks. As usual we laid down our cinder barrage, thinking that this would wipe the white boys out. But they replied with a steady bombardment of broken bottles. We doubled our cinder barrage, but they hid behind trees, hedges, and the sloping embankments of their lawns. Having no such fortifications, we retreated to the brick pillars of our homes. During the retreat a broken milk bottle caught me behind the ear, opening a deep gash which bled profusely.* (p. 21)

Until the initial contact with the "white boys," the central character was quite content with his "cinder environment" and unaware of advantages and disadvantages marked by the color line. Beyond geographical markers—black cinders for blacks and green lawns for whites—what it really meant to be "black" became known when he had to tell his mother about having to be rushed to a hospital (by a neighbor) for stitches behind the ear. Furthermore, Wright (1937/2001) continued:

> *It was all right to throw cinders. The greatest harm a cinder could do was leave a bruise. But broken bottles were dangerous; they left you cut, bleeding, and helpless. When night fell, my mother came from the white folks' kitchen. I raced down the street to meet her. I could just feel in my bones that she would understand. I knew she would tell me exactly what to do next time. I grabbed her hand and babbled out the whole story. She examined my wound, then slapped me. "How come yuh didn't hide?" she asked me. "How come yuh awways fightin'?" I was outraged, and bawled. Between sobs I told her that I didn't have any trees or hedges to hide behind. There wasn't a thing I could have used as a trench. And you couldn't throw very far when you were hiding behind the brick pillars of a house. She grabbed a barrel stave, dragged me home, stripped me naked, and beat me till I had a fever of one hundred and two. She would smack my rump with the stave, and, while the skin was still smarting, impart to me gems of Jim Crow wisdom. I was never to throw cinders any more. I was never to fight any more wars. I was never, never, under any conditions, to fight white folks again. And they were absolutely right in clouting me with the broken milk bottle. Didn't I know she was working hard every day in the hot kitchens of the white folks to make money to take care of me? When was I ever going to learn to be a good boy? She couldn't be bothered with my fights. She finished by telling me that I ought to be thankful to God as long as I lived that they didn't kill me.* (pp. 21–22)

Similarly, in chapters four and five, participants will also express "Jim Crow wisdom" which they heard from parents and teachers and, in turn, passed down to their students and children. Working collaboratively, parents, teachers, and community members tried to protect children from white abuse and the threat of violence. Black children were expected to understand the racial etiquette or special codes (Delaney, 1998) required on both sides of the color line. Like contemporary expressions of "street wisdom," as sociologist Elijah Anderson (1990) pointed out, Jim Crow wisdom is also "largely a state of mind, but it is demonstrated through a person's comportment" (p. 5). Anderson believed that "this perspective allows one to 'see through' public situations, to anticipate what is about to happen based on cues and signals from those one encounters" (p. 5–6). Every adult in the community had the responsibility to train black youth to understand not only the geopolitics of race and racism, but also the geographies of power (Delaney, 1998). That is, across the Jim Crow South, whites were dominant and blacks were subordinate.

What Wright's central character learned cruelly, every black and white southern child learned through formal and informal socialization in homes, schools, churches, and public space (Ritterhouse, 2006). Wright (1937/2001) explained further:

From that time on, the charm of my cinder yard was gone. The green trees, the trimmed hedges, the cropped lawns grew very meaningful, became a symbol. Even today when I think of white folks, the hard, sharp outlines of white houses surrounded by trees, lawns, and hedges are present somewhere in the background of my mind. Through the years, they grew into an overreaching symbol of fear.

It was a long time before I came in close contact with white folks again. We moved from Arkansas to Mississippi. Here we had the good fortune not to live behind the railroad tracks, or close to white neighborhoods. We lived in the very heart of the local Black Belt. There were black churches and black preachers; there were black schools and black teachers; black groceries and black clerics. In fact, everything was so solidly black that for a long time I did not even think of white folks, save in remote and vague terms. But this could not last forever. As one grows older one eats more. One's clothing costs more. When I finished grammar school I had to go to work. My mother could no longer feed and clothe me on her cooking job.

There is but one place where a black boy who knows no trade can get a job. And that's where the houses and faces are white, where the trees, lawns, and hedges are green. My first job was with an optical company in Jackson, Mississippi. The morning I applied I stood straight and neat before the boss, answering all his questions with sharp yessirs and nosirs. I was very careful to pronounce my sirs distinctly, in order that he might know that I was polite, that I knew where I was, and that I knew he was a white man. I wanted that job badly. He looked me over as though he were examining a prize poodle. He questioned me closely about my schooling, being particularly insistent about how

> much mathematics I had had. He seemed very pleased when I told him I had had two years of algebra.
> 'Boy, how would you like to try to learn something around here?' he asked me. 'I'd like it fine, sir,' I said, happy. I had visions of 'working my way up.' Even Negroes have those visions. (pp. 22–23)

The geographical locations and resources allocated to blacks reinforced black inferiority and white superiority. However, as the central character stated, blacks possessed "visions" of uplift (e.g., "working my way up"), respect (e.g., "stood straight and neat before the boss"), and capital (e.g., "had two years of algebra").

Intentionally, I have stopped Wright's narrative at the point of hope and optimism. It is evident that the central character learned enough "Jim Crow wisdom" to get a job which depended upon racial etiquette and cultural signals: "*I was very careful to pronounce my sirs distinctly, in order that he might know that I was polite, that I knew where I was, and that I knew he was a white man.*" But also, he understood the necessity of presenting skills, knowledge, and credentials for even the most menial jobs in the white world: "*He questioned me closely about my schooling . . . He seemed very pleased when I told him I had had two years of algebra.*" Obviously, the central character's spatial conditions changed from his first encounter with the white boys in a game of war and his later encounter with a white employee in the game of life.

THE IMPORTANCE OF "CAPITAL"

What were the mechanisms that allowed for a shift in the central character's spatial, economic, and personal circumstances? In this particular case, I argue, "two years of algebra" and "Jim Crow wisdom" became forms of "capital." If you think about the term capital in the economic sense, then Wright's character was able to use acquired skills and knowledge in a specific field (segregated labor market) as "currency" that could be exchanged for employment. Although his skin color was indeed a strike against him, he possessed capital that would allow him to cross the color line and to become gainfully employed. Pierre Bourdieu (1977, 1986), a French sociologist, expanded the meaning of the term "capital" by arguing that it could manifest itself in various forms. Bourdieu (1986) wrote:

> Depending on the field in which it functions . . . capital can present itself in three fundamental guises: as *economic capital*, which is immediately and directly convertible into money and may be institutionalized in the forms of property rights; as *cultural capital*, which is convertible, on certain conditions, into economic capital and may be institutionalized in the forms of educational qualifications; and as *social capital*,

made up of social obligations ("connections"), which is convertible, in certain conditions, into economic capital and may be institutionalized in the forms of a title of nobility. (p. 244) (Emphasis mine)

In a world of perfect equality, "capital" would benefit everyone. Looking back at Wright's narrative, the central character used the appropriate greetings, "yessir or nosir," which showed that he possessed the cultural capital (e.g., manners and racial etiquette) in a special field (white public space) which led to economic capital (money from employment). Potentially, although it cannot be seen thus far, employment could lead to social capital (personal contacts across the color line that could be used at a later date).

Capital is neither given nor received equally, however. In "Distinction: A Social Critique of the Judgement of Taste," translated by Richard Nice, Bourdieu (1984) made a strong case for undeniable class differences and outcomes based upon the degree to which an individual possesses certain academic credentials in French society. Similarly, in Jim Crow society, the geopolitics of race and racism made it impossible for blacks to make any gains without the possession of "institutionalized" credentials, knowledge, or skills that could be exchanged. In general, blacks needed this form of "cultural capital" in order to succeed. But it must be remembered that blacks could not "embody," possess, or use their "cultural capital" in the same way that whites could due to rules of social interaction in white public space. As Bourdieu (1986) concluded, cultural capital existed in three different states: embodied (long lasting dispositions of the mind and body), objectified (cultural goods such as books, instruments, and machines), and institutionalized (educational qualifications). The social world of Jim Crow demanded that blacks possess a form of cultural capital that maintained their spatial conditions; it also required that blacks acquired a form of institutionalized cultural capital that could be exchanged for jobs. What was this capital that blacks needed for social mobility, while upholding the racial etiquette and cultural norms of "living Jim Crow?"

The answer to this question will unfold in the remaining chapters. Black teachers, I argue, were greatly involved and responsible for the acquisition of this institutionalized form of cultural capital. Yet, some scholars have accused black teachers of lacking a "vision" for the black race and maintaining the status quo of subordination and racial segregation (for a full presentation and critique of this argument, see Fairclough 2001). As Edwards's account illustrated, it is important to remember that white supremacy and geopolitical practices became the superstructure for the social organization of the Jim Crow South. Both demanded a unique consciousness among blacks to know when and where to apply racial etiquette (mispronouncing words to appear ignorant and deferring to whites on the sidewalk, as examples). In public, many blacks—particularly teachers who were hired at the will of the all-white school board—may have appeared to collude with their own subordination. As James Scott (1990) noted, however: "the motives behind acts of deference will remain opaque to us until and unless the power that prompts it weakens or else we can speak confidentially, backstage to those whose motives we wish to understand" (p. 25).

The remaining chapters in this book explore hidden transcripts in the collective remembering among a small number of Jim Crow's teachers many years after the fact. I have traveled throughout three counties in North Carolina in order to go "backstage" and talk with former teachers about what they remember. The real visions and dispositions of black teachers can be revealed through the unveiling of hidden transcripts obtained through oral interviewing and archival research. "The hidden transcripts are created by subordinate groups that critique power covertly, off-stage and beyond direct observation of the dominant groups," as Hamlin (2002) pointed out. Chapters four and five, for example, will show that there is some evidence that the all-black school before integration was an intellectual and social space away from the larger white community. Here blacks could excel without deference to whites or playing the "Nigger" role. However, just as the life of Wright's character was shaped by the geopolitics of race and racism in rural Arkansas, the lives and careers of my participants were shaped by the same social and historical forces in Jim Crow North Carolina. In the final chapter of the book, I will conclude with Wright's narrative about the social meanings of living Jim Crow. In the next chapter, I explore themes from participants' voices of collective remembering which they believed to be important and necessary to understand their visions, motivations, dispositions and actions.

3 Voices of Collective Remembering
Black Teachers in Edgecombe, Nash, and Wilson Counties

Conflict over the quality and character of legally segregated schools for blacks, and its teachers, is more a problem of assessment than a problem of inaccurate accounts. In my own investigation of teachers' work and lives in the all-black school, I have searched for data that would allow me to compare what teachers said then with what they say now. With some research and luck, I found a pioneering study conducted by Frederick A. Rodgers which was published in 1975 as a book entitled, *The Black High School and its Community*. This was a timely and significant study because Rodgers surveyed principals, superintendents, teachers and special staff, students, parents, and community leaders—less than five years after school integration. Rodgers also collected state data that schools reported to the North Carolina Department of Public Instruction (NCDPI) each year.[1]

While the emphasis of his work is on the effects of segregation and desegregation policies on educational practice, the Rodgers study dealt with the schooling experiences of black youth and the work experiences of black teachers. Writing about the all-black school as a social institution, Rodgers reported "statistical summaries" that not only enlighten, but also help to set the record straight about the quality and character of Jim Crow education at the moment of transition into desegregated schools. For example, 97 percent of the principals that he surveyed gave 1972 as the year that the black high school "ceased to operate" (Rodgers, 1975, p. 36). Of course, this date conflicts with the often cited year of school desegregation in the official memory and history—1954.

Moreover, the Rodgers study has proven to be important to my work for many other reasons:

1. He focused on segregation and desegregation data from North Carolina, specifically eastern North Carolina, which is the same geographic region that I study.[2]
2. He compiled statistics on the all-black high school and the all-white school using state data from multiple sources.

3. He collected interview data with twenty black principals and twenty white superintendents.[3]
4. He administered questionnaires to five groups of people, directly connected to the all-black high school: principals, teachers and special staff, parents, students, and community leaders.[4]

It is a great fortune that I came across the Rodgers study, conducted approximately three to five years after an overwhelming majority of all-black schools had integrated in North Carolina. One can only imagine the luxury of interviewing major players in the drama of school integration in Edgecombe, Nash, and Wilson Counties, especially now since many of them are no longer living.

The Rodgers study is perhaps one of the first attempts to uncover the intended and unintended consequences of school integration for black educators. For instance, Rodgers (1975) reported: "In 1963–64, of the 226 principals of black schools that included high school grades, twenty-four served as principals of senior high schools (grades 9–12 or 10–12), twenty-three served as principals of junior-senior high schools (grades 5–12, 6–12, 7–12, or 8–12), and the remaining 179 served as principals of union high schools (grades 1–12). Ten years after, there were *fifteen* black principals serving in schools with grades 10 and/or above. . . . The principals were located in fourteen different counties and fifteen different administrative units" (p. 70). (Emphasis mine). Although I focus on black teachers more so than black principals in my study, these statistics provide a clear geospatial picture given that the number of principals dropped from 226 to 15 (Rodgers, 1975, p. 70). Shifting the focus to teachers, according to Cecelski (1994), "North Carolina was second only to Texas in the number of jobs lost by black teachers: by 1972, an estimated 3,051 blacks in North Carolina had lost teaching jobs after the merger of black and white schools" (p. 8).

Michele Foster (1997) came across a hidden transcript made public in an official communiqué in 1965 from the National Education Association (NEA), entitled "Task Force Survey of Displacement in Seventeen Southern States," which explains the geopolitical practice of dismissing and displacing black educators.[5] The 1965 NEA task force declared:

> It is clear that in the past, Negro teachers were employed specifically and exclusively for the purpose of teaching Negro pupils in segregated schools. Segregated schools required segregated facilities. Since Negro teachers were employed to teach Negro pupils, there were relatively few positions for Negro teachers in a school system with few classes for Negroes. In a system with no classes for Negroes, there were simply no positions for Negro teachers. It has been, and still is, widely assumed by many school board members that Negroes, both students and teachers, are intellectually inferior. From this specious premise, it follows

that 'quality education' can be obtained only when schools, even after being integrated, remain in spirit and often in name 'white schools.' White schools are viewed as having no place for Negro teachers." (Foster, 1997, p. xxxviii–xxxvix)

Today, it is very hard to imagine that a high profile task force representing the largest teachers' association in the United States would make such a statement about black schools and teachers. However, it must be remembered that the time in which this statement was made public, the majority of white educational authorities thought that all black institutions—from schools to churches to banks—were inferior and ineffective (Sokol, 2006).

In this chapter, I present the voices of collective remembering among participants in my study to compare what they remember to the information in archives and secondary historical sources. I have chosen four themes which emerged from the data. More importantly, each of these themes appeared as "privileged" background information, "off the record" comments, or "you must remember this" anecdotes. The more provocative "off the record" comments, I have kept in a special file with an agreement with participants to never "let white people know all our secrets." This need to filter accounts, stories, and memories reveals just how delicate an issue it is when the hidden transcript is revealed, even after all these years have passed (Scott, 1990; Hamlin, 2002). The Rodgers study allowed me to further investigate the more provocative comments and statements recorded in oral interviews. For example, participants stated that black teachers were much more qualified than white teachers in North Carolina—which I will explore later in this chapter. With the Rodgers study in hand, I have a "composite view of the black high school based on official public data and the expressed perceptions of participants connected directly and indirectly with the ongoing activities of the [all-black] institution" (p. xi).

I use findings from Rodgers' questionnaires, state data collection, and archival materials to verify and to support participants' voices of collective remembering. In this way, as participants lay out the geopolitical realities which shaped their work as classroom teachers, I can compare just how near or far the accounts that I have collected are from those Rodgers collected. One of the limitations of the Rodgers study was explained in great detail: "The State Department discontinued the practice of collecting separate data on black and white schools at the close of the 1963–1964 school year. It was therefore decided that that year should serve as a boundary line period for collecting, collating, analyzing, summarizing, and evaluating the data that described the black high school as a dynamic operating unit" (p. 102). Given that 1963–1964 is the last year that separate data on blacks, whites, and Indians in North Carolina schools, the Rodgers study provides a view into the perceptions, functions and activities of black principals and teachers before desegregation. Common themes emerged across three counties more than forty years since the close of participants' school workplaces.

FARMING GEOGRAPHIES

Edgecombe, Wilson, and Nash counties are located in the coastal plain region of North Carolina. Historically, this region has been an agricultural leader in the production of tobacco, cotton, and peanuts in North Carolina. In the region's rural communities, the black public schools faced extraordinary disadvantages because of seasonal agricultural work and the demand for children's labor. The Rodgers (1975) study explained: "allocations for per pupil expenditure were made on the basis of attendance figures taken in the early fall, right in the middle of the harvest. Many black children were needed at home during this time" (p. 52). Educational historian James Anderson (1988) noted a significant decline in the use of black child labor in rural Southern communities by the 1930s due to the migration of farm families to urban centers. Participants in my study, however, stated that the practice continued well into the 1980s. For example, Equiller Lucas, who started teaching in Edgecombe County in 1964, remembered:

> I had a 4th grade class in a rural school. They had very large families and sharecropping was the main occupation in that area. They were eager to learn but they were out of school a lot because they had to work on the farm. Mainly, they had peanuts and tobacco. . . . I would always encourage them to stay in school, but parents would write notes saying that they would be out next week because 'we got to get up peas.' I was thinking that they were talking about field peas, but they were talking about peanuts. I ate a lot of peanuts those years [laughing] because students would bring back peanuts to school."

"Even if allocations were made fairly," as Rodgers (1975) reasoned, "with all other things being equal, the total amount of money received per pupil by black high schools came to a smaller percentage . . . than was justified by attendance during the school year, excluding the early fall. And, of course, many black schools, which were at the mercy of the central office, did not receive even the share of funds to which they were entitled" (p. 52).

Participants recalled the unintended consequences of seasonal farm work. That is, the harsh life on the farm actually motivated them to graduate from high school and to continue on to college. Susie Branford reflected, "I'll tell you why I went to college. We worked on a farm and it could get mighty hot out there. And I told my sister one day when we were suckering tobacco that I'm not going to do this for the rest of my life. That was hard work! And, the teachers use to wear such pretty clothes. I thought that if I get to be a teacher, I can do that too." Likewise, Josephine Edwards stated, "My goal was to get off the farm. . . . I didn't want to think about living on a farm the rest of my life. [I thought] there has to be something better." Another participant remarked that working on the farm not only motivated him to become a teacher, but also underscored his pedagogical and advising repertoire. Roosevelt Pitt remembered:

> At that time, they were telling kids to get out of high school. And, we will talk about college when you get to high school. There were so many dropping out. See, you have to realize that it was a farming area and the white man owned everything. . . . In the middle of the year when crops started coming off, we would put kids on the bus next to the window to make it look like the bus was full—that's how bad it was. But farming was the only thing they could do: 'I got to feed my kids and my kids got to work so that we can feed the family and after that they can go back to school.' That's why we were preaching, 'I don't care what you have to do, get out of high school.' You can always find some money to go to college later on in life.

These accounts uncover hidden responses to a geopolitical practice (black child labor in seasonal agricultural work) that I will address in later chapters.

According to participants, most parents were intentional in their efforts to encourage children to chart out new territory and opportunities with a high school or college education. The Rodgers (1975) study provides some additional support to this claim: "Of the principals reporting, 45 percent felt that approximately 50 to 75 percent of the parents were interested in their children obtaining good grades" (p. 36). Reflecting upon her schooling experience, Lucille Edwards recalled that "even though my mother was a seasonal worker [and worked as a domestic], her philosophy was 'I want more for my children than what I have accomplished' so therefore she pushed. And, that's how I got into college—not knowing whether I was going to stay there or where the money would come from." In another example, Gloria Gray explained that her parents "pushed" education despite pressures to keep their children in the fields: "My parents were tenant farmers. They had this rule that we could not stay out of school. There were so many children who would stay out of school to pick cotton and I begged my mother to stay out of school. And finally, she let me and I think I picked 30 lbs of cotton and she promised to whip me if I ever asked her again. So, we were not allowed to stay out of school—under no circumstances." While I am not certain the number of parents who took similar stances as Lucille Edward's and Gloria Gray's parents, their accounts indicate that there were different and complex responses from teachers and parents to seasonal agricultural work which depended upon black child labor.

THE ABSENCE OF WHITE PEOPLE

Interviews uncovered that white people were totally absent in the daily life of teaching and learning in legally segregated schools for blacks. "The black principal had the most contact with white educational authorities," according to the Rodgers study (1975). Moreover, Rodgers gave a qualitative report of the "professional contact" between the black principal, the white superintendent, and the white community:

> The black principal often had no real idea what was going on at the white schools . . . Often when the superintendent met with the black principal, he met with him alone, and the principal would have no idea what white principals were being told by the central office. These meetings were rare, and rarer still were visits to the schools from anyone in the central office. Quite frequently the [all-white] central office was not even aware that black schools had yearbooks, and they cared little what was included in programs of instruction. Said one principal: "As long as we prepared you to dig a straight ditch and cook a good meal, and you didn't blow up the building . . . that was all they were concerned about." (p. 54)

More than forty years later, Maureen Brown recalled, "Coming from an all-black school, an all-black situation, or an all-black setting—over here and over there. I never even thought about over there because I was concentrating on this over here—which [was] all-black. And, I would hear of Coon and Fike (former all-white schools in Wilson County, North Carolina), but that was just the scope of it. I knew that I didn't belong there, so it didn't bother me."

Likewise, Athalene Emory reflected, "We didn't know what was going on in the white community—we had our students. I guess what we were doing was trying to say okay when you graduate from here you are going to be in a bigger society and you need to be able to fit into it and you are going to have to compete." There is a consensus that the all-black school existed in its own social world with little to no interaction with white educational authorities, students, teachers, and community members. However, Emory's comment betrays the very notion of "total absence" when she implied that her concentration was on preparing students for "a bigger society" in which black children would "have to compete." More importantly, Emory's comment raises more questions about the subtle and unconscious ways in which whiteness (people, culture, structure, and ideas) shaped some teachers' pedagogical motivations and decisions. How might caring and uplifting teachers, like Emory, have been unconsciously structured and organized by the geopolitics of race and racism?

The spatial realities of Jim Crow did present moments of "contact" between blacks and whites outside of the schoolhouse gates. Since Frederick

Rodger's (1975) study interviewed white principals just a few years after schools were integrated, he was able to establish that "the white principals did not seem to know much about what was happening in the black schools, in spite of the fact that they often said that they enjoyed a good relationship with the black administrators" (p. 56). While participants in my study also stated that they did not know much about the all-white school and its community, some participants did recall concrete incidents of a "bad relationship" with whites in public space. Recounting an incident that she believed would always be implanted into her memory, for example, Mildred Hines remarked:

> I will never forget how we would come out to the road to catch the bus. [White children] would see us coming and form a line, so that we would have to jump into the ditch to get to the bus. . . . I remember I had a little raincoat and a hat that my mama bought me. And, I remember very well that [a white boy] saw me and [he] jumped in mud so that it would get all over my coat. I cried. But there was a white girl on the bus—my mama ironed for them—she was so mad that she reported it when she got to school. I remember those kinds of things.

Another example came from Gloria Burks who also described incidents of violence in the street on the way home from school: "When they came up from Kenan Street and hit Broad Street, we were coming along Broad Street to come home too. . . . They would say nigger and that's it! And you would come home many days being scraped up—that is why I learned to fight." Both Hines and Burks spoke about the violent interactions away from the all-black school in white public space. Remember also that Hines spoke about the "white girl on the bus" who reported her white male classmate when she arrived to school. (The girl must have felt sympathy for the ironing woman's child, as Hines had never interacted with the girl before the incident.) Clearly, these accounts point to mostly "bad relationships" between the races but even positive accounts, like the "good relationships" that the white administrators reported in the Rodgers study, are complicated by unequal power relations.

In legally segregated schools for blacks, whites were indeed "present" through the geopolitics of race and racism. In *Balm in Gilead*, a biographical account of a pioneering black female psychoanalysis and medical doctor, Sara Lawrence-Lightfoot (1995) has articulated what it meant to always be in the presence of whiteness even when white people were not physically around:

> "Like many cities and towns in the Deep South, the residential segregation did not appear to be clearly drawn. That is, neighborhoods were often inhabited by both blacks and whites, the races living side by side. But this apparent color mixture was misleading. It did not reflect

integration or easy relationships across color lines. It reflected the fact that the southern psyche had so fully incorporated the caste system between races that there was no need for geographic boundaries. The map of segregation resided in the minds of blacks and whites, and there was no need to draw it on the land" (p. 48).

The power of white people to totally control what occurred in the all-black school should not be over-emphasized, however.

Some parents resisted white domination. For example, Gloria Gray remembered an occasion when "the crops were coming off" and the landowner wanted her dad to keep his children out of school: "My dad said that he was not going to let us [miss school] . . . When we got home from school, we would go to the fields to work. He told my dad that if you don't do what I tell you, I will kick you. I remember that my dad said, "no you won't and if you do, you will regret it." And, we moved at the end of that farming year. I don't know if this was a direct consequence, because I had heard my parents talk about it before, but we built our own home." Some blacks could control the physical absence or presence of white people in their lives, but the social psychological presence of whiteness had been woven into the social fabric of the Jim Crow South. Subsequent chapters will offer examples of resistance and mediated action by teachers.

QUALIFIED TEACHERS OVER HERE

In their history of public school reform, educational historians David Tyack and Larry Cuban (1995) gave a rather negative impression of the quality of black schools, in general, and an even worse one of black teachers. Tyack and Cuban wrote:

> In 1940 about two out of three blacks lived in rural areas, overwhelmingly in the South. Racial oppression compounded inequalities created by the poverty of the region. Disenfranchised blacks had to make do with the starvation diet of school funds that white officials allocated to the segregated 'colored' schools. Blacks constituted over a quarter of the public school students but received only 12 percent of revenues. *Half of the black teachers had gone no further than high school, compared with 7 percent of white teachers.* They often lacked the most basic aids to learning–textbooks, slates, and chalk, or desks–and frequently had very large classes when the children were not needed for farm labor. (p. 23) (Emphasis mine)

When you consider the italicized sentence about the scholastic training of black teachers and their working conditions before integration, it is no small wonder why black teachers have been remembered so negatively.

This "official" story about black teachers in legally segregated schools for blacks supports a negative collective memory. Close examination of Tyack and Cuban's footnotes reveal that this quotation was made in reference to a single East Texas school before the 1940s from a "visitor" to the school (Tyack and Cuban, 1995, p. 151). While this assessment may have been true for this one school in East Texas, it probably was not true of all segregated schools for blacks in East Texas or throughout the state.

The former teachers I interviewed reported that black teachers in North Carolina were certified across the board. This was a consistent message in my interviews.[6] These findings are supported by a wave of counter-narratives by scholars in history and education of "the good all-black school" and "exemplary black teachers" before school integration, focusing particularly on North Carolina's black public schools and teachers (See Cecelski, 1994; Dempsey and Noblit, 1993; Noblit and Dempsey, 1996; Fairclough, 2001; Foster, 1990, 1991, 1993, 1997; Jeffries, 1994; McCullough-Garrett, 1993; Philipsen, 1993, 1999; Siddle-Walker, 1996a, 1996b). In my study, for example, Alton Bobbitt remembered:

> We had a survey of teacher certification and the superintendent came over to Frederick Douglass [School] and said, 'I should not be over here talking about certification because the principal has a master's degree, there are 42 people on this faculty and out of that 42, there are 17 master's degrees here,' and everything else was A certificates. . . . This was in 1964. And, he said I should not even be over here. I should go back to Elm City High School (the white school) where we have people with nonstandard certification, B certificates, C certificates, and no degrees." But they were still teaching.

In Bobbitt's account, the racial landscape is divided—black teachers "over here," white teachers "over there." Contrary to popular belief, Bobbitt claimed that black teachers were over-qualified on the black side of town in comparison to white teachers. Adding some support, Elmer Cummings, a former teacher, counselor, and principal, recalled:

> At that time, we did not have a shortage of black teachers. In fact we were over supplied with black teachers. We had a surplus of black teachers because that was the only thing that most of us could go into. They went on and got their masters, doctorates, and things like that. The supply of white teachers wasn't that great, so they were hiring teachers with B certificates.

If Tyack and Cuban are correct, then my teachers' memories and impressions might be incorrect. The Rodgers study and my own exploration of state data allowed me to explore this matter further.

In North Carolina, the Rodgers (1975) study found that "by 1947–48 the quality of teacher training and preparation for blacks and whites was reversed from what it had been in 1924–25. In fact, from 1941 to 1948, the number of white teachers teaching on non-standard certificates rose from 1022 to 2909, while the numbers of black teachers holding 'A' standard certificates went from 5806 to 6240" (p. 32). Following Rodger's lead, I searched the archives at the North Carolina Collection on the campus of the University of North Carolina at Chapel Hill for data from the North Carolina State Department of Public Instruction (NCDPI). As I explored the Tyack and Cuban thesis further, I found that in 1939–1940, North Carolina teachers had a total index of training of 776.4, with white and black teachers having a separate score of 785.7 and 752.6, respectively (North Carolina State School Facts, July 1941).[7] For both blacks and whites, the number of teachers with "4 years college" training increased tremendously from 1929–30 to 1939–40. The NCDPI reported that there were 47 white teachers and 182 Negro teachers in the state of North Carolina having no college training (North Carolina State School Facts, July 1941). In addition, the data show that 88.8% of white teachers and 67.8% of black teachers were college graduates in 1939–1940.

According to Rodgers' (1975) statistical summary, "In 1923–24, all of ten years after the first public [black] high schools were opened there were fourteen public and twenty private accredited black high schools. These accredited schools served 87 percent of the black students enrolled in high school at the time. Ten years later, 1933–34, there were 106 public and ten private accredited black high schools serving almost 98 percent of blacks enrolled in high school" (p. 30). Between 1937–1939, there were 203 black public high schools and 743 white public high schools in North Carolina, while there were 2, 174 black public elementary schools and 1, 884 white elementary schools (North Carolina State Facts, July 1941). The percentage gap between the number of college graduates for blacks and whites, I argue, can be partially explained by the smaller number of black high schools prior to the mid-1930s (Rodgers, 1975; Anderson, 1988; Perkins, 1989). Since high school departments were just beginning to become commonplace in rural black communities in North Carolina, it makes sense that there were fewer black teachers who had college level preparation to teach in the public schools. The majority of black teachers would have taught in primary and grammar schools, where low levels of scholastic training were expected (Rodgers, 1975; Anderson 1988). Once more public high schools opened and the college degree was a requirement for elementary teachers, then the percentage gap in scholastic training became smaller over time.

Interpretations of percentage gaps in scholastic training (which were smaller than the exaggerations read in history texts) have been used as evidence of black inferiority. I view the percentage gaps as evidence of racism and discrimination in the building and funding of black high schools, and offers little to no insight about the quality of the teachers themselves.[8]

Rodgers (1975) found that "teacher preparation continued to improve until by 1949–50 it surpassed that of white teachers" (p. 32).[9] Likewise, Siddle Walker (2001) documented that, by the 1940s, "the professional preparation of African American teachers began to increase noticeably, and in some cases surpassed that of Whites" (p. 765). Of special note, however, the North Carolina Civil Rights Advisory Committee reported in the *Durham Morning Herald* on October 2, 1960 that Negro teacher salaries were higher than white teacher salaries, even though "'the average Negro income [was] approximately one-half the average white'" (North Carolina Collection Archives). According to the Advisory Committee, "one of the reasons for the difference has been that more Negro teachers hold higher certificates, more Negro teachers remain in their teaching jobs for longer periods of time, thus building up longevity pay" (North Carolina Collection Archives).[10] As early as 1960, the hidden transcript had been revealed in the local Durham newspaper yet neglected in the dominant collective memory.

"Public" records actually confirmed what I had been told in oral history interviews many decades later. When you consider the few employment options that black teachers had, due to the geopolitics of race and racism in Jim Crow North Carolina, the likelihood of a surplus of black teachers seems plausible. All things being equal, black principals, or the white superintendent in some areas, could almost hand-pick the best applicants. In this study, it might be important to note, all of the participants had college degrees when they started teaching and all met the standards for teacher certification that applied to them.[11]

TEACHER POSITIONING

Of the black principals that Rodgers (1975) surveyed, almost half had six to fifteen years teaching experience; 88% were born in North Carolina; 43 percent grew up in rural areas; 93% of the principals had obtained master's degrees; and, 7 percent had only the bachelor's degree.[12] From these data, it can be assumed that teaching was a stepping stone for many black principals, that they tended to be native North Carolinians from rural areas, and that they were probably among the most highly credentialed black person in town. Significantly, the Rodgers (1975) study noted, "the black principal was usually the highest-paid man, the high-status individual in the black community, and his power extended through both the school and the community as a whole" (p. 57). As one white superintendent reflected upon the black principals under his watch: "The faculty was pretty well dominated, the student body was dominated, and the parents were pretty well dominated" (Rodgers, 1975, p. 57). Perhaps in another life and under different circumstances, the highly educated black principal might have chosen a different career.

Within black society, especially in small rural communities, the teaching profession was seen typically as a respectable and honorable profession among middle and upper class blacks; teaching was also an occupation which allowed social mobility for poor and working class blacks (Shaw, 1996). This raises several important questions in research on black teachers before school integration: How did they envision and embrace teaching in the Age of Jim Crow? How did their socioeconomic backgrounds shape their pedagogical practices? Valid answers to these questions must consider the limited occupational structure for college-educated and talented young black people. There were usually only two or three black principals in a school district that could be hired, even fewer in union schools with grades 1-12. Under these circumstances, how did these black teachers approach a craft with little room for upward mobility?

Many participants said that they did not aspire to become teachers. As Rodgers (1975) confirmed, "blacks had little choices in type of employment, with most jobs simply closed to them on the basis of race and with those jobs available drastically underpaid, teaching offered not only something approaching a living wage, but high status in the black community as well" (p. 29). In some cases, parents chose the teaching profession for their daughter or son because it was considered respectable professional work. Other participants desired different careers but somehow ended up "teaching school:"

> I wanted to be a social worker. I just loved people and I wanted to help somebody. My room was the welfare room. People would give me clothes and different things for the children. . . . that was a part of my life that I put into my classroom [pause] being a social worker, not just in my classroom but other classrooms [throughout the school].
>
> (Arcenia Hines)

> When I went to college I did not want to be a teacher. I never did. It is interesting that I spent 30 or more years doing something [pause] I never intended to do back then. But when I went to college, the top profession for African American students was a teacher. I really wanted to be a lawyer . . . but I knew that there was no place. I didn't know any African American attorneys, and females, at that time. So, that just cut me off right at the knees!
>
> (Dianne Turner)

> I wanted to be a secretary. . . . My mother and the principal of the school were determined that everybody who could go was going to college. Well [the principal] was a Shaw [University] grad. He went to Shaw, got all the forms, brought them back, and he filled them out with my mother. . . . I went on to Shaw.
>
> (Hazel Lewis)

Although some teachers did not choose teaching as a first career, they found the work to be rewarding and fulfilling. Despite the fact that she did not become a professional social worker, Arcenia Hines positioned herself as a social welfare agent for the entire school. Dianne Turner channeled her natural talents for research and argumentation into an inspiring career as a history teacher and guidance counselor. And, Hazel Lewis provided decades of unpaid service to her elementary school as the part-time secretary and bookkeeper. These individual lives suggest that highly educated teachers who possessed dreams other than becoming teachers possibly brought unacknowledged creativity, talent, and skills to teaching and learning in the all-black school.

Nevertheless, interviews revealed that teachers had to be cautious about their ideas and their "place" in rural black and white southern communities. On the one hand, teachers had to be able to interact with and to get along with members of the larger black community outside of the school. On the other hand, black teachers had to follow the local racial etiquette established by the white community outside of the school. In the first situation, within the black community, some participants mentioned how blacks believed that "too much education" could be a bad thing. At the same time that parents pushed their sons and daughters to graduate from high school or to attend college, they also feared that a college education could break a child's bond to family and community. In his interview, for example, Roosevelt Pitt echoed this point as he recalled what his father often told him as a young boy: "If you're educated and can't talk to a kid that is not educated, then my daddy would say that you are an 'educated fool.' That's exactly how he put it. 'If you go to school, Roosevelt, and get a degree, don't become an 'educated fool.'"

Similarly, Du Bois (1903/1994) wrote about this "problem" within rural black communities in "Of the Coming of John," a chapter in the *Souls of Black Folks*. Briefly, Du Bois' central character, John, returns home from college to teach but feels estranged from the "natives" as he questions their old religion and country ways: "The people were distinctly bewildered. This silent, cold man—was this John? Where was his smile and hearty hand-grasp? "'Peared kind o' down in the mouf," said the Methodist preacher thoughtfully. "Seemed monstus stuck up," complained a Baptist sister" (p. 183). At issue, I argue, was the fact that black teachers had to possess a "spirit of connectedness" to the community rather than a "spirit of alienation."

Within the white community, the geopolitics of race and racism demanded that black teachers respect the rules for social interaction set by the dominant white community. For instance, in "Of the Coming of John," Du Bois (1903/1994) wrote about the day in which John approached the [white] judge about teaching:

> You've come for the school, I suppose. Well, John, I want to speak to you plainly. You know I'm a friend to your people. I've helped you and your

> family, and would have done more if you hadn't got the notion of going off. Now I like the colored people, and sympathize with all the reasonable aspirations; but you and I both know, John, that in this country the Negro must remain subordinate, and can never expect to be the equal of white men. In their place, your people can be honest and respectful; and God knows, I'll do what I can to help them. But when they want to reverse nature, and rule white men . . . Now, John, the question is, are you, with your education and Northern notions, going to accept the situation and teach the darkies to be faithful servants and laborers as your fathers were . . . or are you going to try to put fool ideas of rising and equality into these folks' heads, and make them discontented and unhappy?" (pp. 186–187)

Similar to the position that John faced after returning to the South with a college degree, some participants stated that they received their first teaching position in their hometown after a white person "vouched" for them. Other participants reported that they obtained their first job as a result of their parents' social networks—either working for a white person or "knowing somebody who knew somebody" on the school board. First and foremost, participants stated that they had to "qualify" for the job, but oftentimes they had to be "looked over" for approval. While it is clear that parents wanted to have their daughter or son home and connected to their community, participants also believed that parents knew that social codes demanded that professional positions for blacks be negotiated with white educational authorities, as well as the black principal.

Helen Toney remembered that although she had been offered a job in the city of Charlotte, North Carolina, she began teaching in her hometown because her father secured her a job through several conversations with the white superintendent. Similar to Toney, Pauline White recalled that her mother secured her a teaching job while taking care of the white superintendent's ailing niece, at the time in which she was finishing coursework at Winston-Salem State Teachers College. Repeating what her mother told her, White restated what the superintendent said:

> As well as you are taking care of my niece, you make sure she sends an application to me. Better still, maybe I can see her and talk with her when she comes home for Christmas.'

White remembers going to the hospital to meet the superintendent, who asked her very few questions and said:

> 'You look like a person who would want to work at a little country school.' . . . He said, 'your mother told me this.'

Not only did White begin her teaching career in a 2-room school close near home, she spent her entire teaching career in that school district. Like

White, other participants said that they received their first teaching job because they were "hometown girls" or "hometown boys" in the eyes of white educational authorities. It should also be noted that quite a few participants stated that they did not get jobs, although they had lived in the same town all of their life (except the college years), because they were from the "wrong family" or the "wrong section of town." These participants claimed that some teaching jobs were saved for the sons and daughters of the black middle class. While there is no way of really knowing whether or not these assertions are "true," in the next chapter I explore these inter- and intra-racial struggles so that even these disconfirming accounts can be told and remembered.

Part II
Hidden Transcripts Revealed

4 "The Way We Found Them to Be"
Black Teachers and the Politics of Respectability in Jim Crow North Carolina

Despite a growing educational literature about the quality and character of legally segregated schools for blacks, the dominant and wide-spread view assumes that before school integration blacks were intellectually unequal to whites due to inferior education. I encountered this in a class I taught at a state university when I showed segments from the award-winning civil rights documentary series, *Eyes on the Prize* (Hampton, 1986). When I asked for verbal reactions to footage from the 1960s, one white student remarked: "I was shocked that the black people were so articulate, more than some of the whites!" Other students (black and white) said that they too had been surprised. This chapter has been inspired by these students and seeks to reclaim the legacy of Jim Crow's teachers.

In the dominant collective memory of segregated schooling, as education historian Vanessa Siddle Walker (1996) noted: "Southern African-Americans were victims of whites who questioned the utility of providing blacks with anything more than a rudimentary education ... The children suffered immeasurably and, the memory assumes, received little of educational value until they were desegregated into the superior white systems" (p. 1). Similarly, educational anthropologist Michele Foster (1997) remarked that "part of the problem lay in the *Brown* decision, which rested on the assumption that a school with an all-black faculty did not provide an education equal to that provided by an all-white faculty even if the buildings and equipment were superior" (p. xxxv). At every educational level, students today enter and leave their schooling experience with a textually mediated memory of the "all-black school" as intellectually barren and inherently inferior.

Perhaps less dominant in the national consciousness, but central in academic discourses, black teachers themselves have been accused of being more concerned with their own status than they were with educating students or advancing black rights (Frazier, 1957; Rist, 1970; for a detailed discussion, see Fairclough, 2001). In *Black Bourgeoisie*—an American Sociological Association award-winning book—sociologist E. Franklin Frazier (1957) indicted black teachers as members of the black bourgeoisie for "[having] shown no interest in the 'liberation' of Negroes except as it affected their own status or acceptance by the white community" (p. 235). Furthermore, Frazier declared:

> ... the present [Negro] teachers have little interest in 'making men,' but are concerned primarily with teaching as a source of income which will enable them to maintain middle-class standards and participate in Negro 'society.' It appears that the majority of them have no knowledge of books nor any real love of literature. Today many of the teachers of English and literature never read a book as a source of pleasure or recreation. (p. 81)

Frazier rejected the notion that "bourgeois" black teachers were qualified, resourceful, and dedicated professionals. In his indictment of black teachers as preoccupied with both "status" and "acceptance by whites," Frazier clearly linked black teachers to negative aspects of the culture of respectability. That is, he claimed that black teachers thought of themselves as a "better class" of blacks, emphasized morals and manners to eradicate white racism, and employed respectability through "service to the masses" (Gaines, 1996, p. xiv).

To date, there have been two main positions concerning segregated schools and the black teachers who taught in them. On the one hand, the dominant narrative maintains that segregated schools for blacks were inferior schools, and its teachers were inadequate and concerned primarily with their own status. On the other hand, the counter-narrative emphasizes black teachers' cultural responses to structural constraints and white racism in the "good" all-black school, and the ways their responses were rooted in black culture. I offer a third position which reconsiders elements of both.

I contend that black teachers worked toward racial uplift and that their efforts were as political as they were cultural. As Beauboeuf-Lafontant (1999) stated, "The political clarity of generations of black teachers is, I believe, less a reflection of culture and more an embodiment of these educators' personal and political commitments" (p. 717). Like Beauboeuf-Lafontant, I investigate "the political nature of racial uplift" (p. 711). The first position argues that black teachers considered themselves a "better class," while the second position might be characterized as approaching a view of "race with no class." My own position focuses on "race and class" through a look at how the politics of respectability shaped black teachers' work before school integration.[1]

I present my position with an overview and formulation of some relevant literatures about both respectability and black teachers in the Age of Jim Crow. Next, I present research findings based primarily on my discovery of hidden transcripts in oral interviews with teachers in three counties in North Carolina. The findings are organized around three of five themes taken from a comprehensive historiography of black teachers from 1940-1960, published by Siddle Walker (2001): 1. Relating the curriculum to students' needs; 2. Caring about students; and 3. Developing a relationship with the community. In each corresponding section, I show how the politics of respectability shaped teachers' perceptions and actions.

THE POLITICS OF RESPECTABILITY

At the turn of the 20th century, "respectability" loomed large in the personal and professional lives of the black elite and middle classes (Gilmore, 1996; Higginbotham, 1993; McHenry, 2002; Perkins, 1983; Shaw, 1996; Wolcott, 2001). "Respectability demanded that every individual in the black community assume responsibility for behavioral self-regulation and self-improvement along moral, educational, and economic lines; the goal was to distance oneself as far as possible from images perpetuated by racist stereotypes," as historian Evelyn Brooks Higginbotham (1993; p. 196) noted. In the early days of racial uplift through "bourgeois respectability," members of the black elite and middle classes created educational and social institutions that emphasized "being respectable" for poor and working-class blacks (Higginbotham, 1993; McHenry, 2002; Shaw, 1996). In practice, respectability meant different things to different people, such as Booker T. Washington's notions of "industrial education," W. E. B Du Bois' ideas of a "Talented Tenth," Nannie Helen Burroughs' push for "Bible, Bath, and Broom," and Anna Julia Cooper's call for "elevated and trained womanhood" (Du Bois, 1903/2002; Gaines, 1996; May, 2007; Wolcott, 1997).

Many black elite and middle class professionals reasoned that the underdeveloped black majority needed to be "raised" or "uplifted" out of their circumstances as formerly enslaved people in order to be accepted by mainstream white society (Litwack, 1998; McHenry, 2002; Shaw, 1996). Some black reformers were faced with the "contradictory task of using uplift ideology to expose the moral bankruptcy of white supremacy while seeking the recognition and cooperation of white reformers and philanthropic and business elites" (Gaines, 1996, p. 133). But as Kevin Gaines (1996) warned:

> It is crucial to realize that uplift ideology was not simply a matter of educated African Americans wanting to be white, as E. Franklin Frazier's polemic attacking a materialistic, status-addicted black bourgeoisie suggested. On the contrary, uplift ideology also represented the struggle for a positive black identity in a deeply racist society, turning the pejorative designation of race into a source of dignity and self-affirmation through an ideology of class differentiation, self-help, and interdependence" (p. 3).

My perspective on black teachers has been greatly influenced by Gaines' insights, which has led me to rethink the negative function of a politics of respectability within black life and culture during the Jim Crow years. Clearly, sociologist E. Franklin Frazier connected black teachers to an elite identity, which emphasized good behavior, status and reputation. Even if Frazier accurately described some group of black teachers before integration, there is mounting evidence that other teachers drew upon a respectability discourse to foster a sense of purpose and of hope in legally segregated schools for blacks (Fairclough, 2001; Foster, 1997; Siddle Walker, 1996).

Historian Victoria Wolcott (2001) has argued convincingly that "[bourgeois respectability] was undermined during the Great Depression when the realities of economic survival" challenged black leaders and their institutions (p. 242). For example, the Great Depression worked a "special hardship on southern black schools" which often took away "the barest essentials in the educational program, including the teacher," as Franklin and Moss (1994, p. 407) explained. Consequently, some members of the black elite and middle class emphasized "economic nationalism and civil rights" and called for "rights to a living wage, self-defense, and equality" (Wolcott, 2001, p. 242). By the end of WWII, black elite and middle class reformers shifted their focus away from "bourgeois respectability" and emphasized "civil rights and social power." The black teachers I interviewed started teaching after World War II during a time in which respectability had been reshaped and reformulated into a broader vision of racial uplift beyond morals and manners.

BLACK TEACHERS BEFORE INTEGRATION

Dominant accounts of Jim Crow teaching and learning are profoundly negative. Consequently, as chapter 1 explained, scholars have begun to reconstruct a counter-narrative of the "good" or "valued" segregated school before integration (Beauboeuf-Lafontant, 1999, 2002; Cecelski, 1994; Chafe, Gavins, & Korstad, 2001; Dougherty, 1998; Fairclough, 2000, 2001, 2004; Foster, 1990, 1991, 1993, 1997; Jeffries, 1994; Noblit and Dempsey, 1996; Philipsen, 1999; Randolph, 2004; Siddle Walker, 1996a, 1996b, 2000, 2001, 2004; Watkins, 2001; White, 2004). To review briefly, as early as the mid-1960s, there was a conscious effort among former students and teachers to remember the "good" all-black school that existed before federally-mandated public school desegregation (Hundley, 1965; Jones, 1981; Sowell, 1976; Morris & Morris, 2002). Some scholars argue that these memories are merely nostalgic (e.g., Shircliffe, 2001), while I contend that these memories are the unveiling of hidden transcripts (Scott, 1990)—latent reports of the social world created and lived in the all-black school before integration.

Just as scholars have critiqued the dominant narrative and memory of legally segregated schools for blacks as skewed toward the negative, emphasizing only the lack of resources and of financial equality, counter-narratives are generally skewed toward the positive, overemphasizing culture (understood as race) and community (e.g., Foster, 1990, 1991, 1993; Irvine, 1989; Siddle Walker, 2004). Clearly, the late E. Franklin Frazier (1957) was a contributor to this dominant understanding of segregated black schools as inferior, with his image of teachers as caring more about their own status than about student learning. Within the counter-narrative, which has focused on teacher responses to structural constraints and white racism, Michele Foster and Vanessa Siddle Walker are two of the most significant and substantial contributors. Unlike Frazier, however, both Foster and Siddle Walker have spent their entire careers researching the lives and work of black teachers. They have sought to counter the historical image and record of black teachers as "uncaring, unsympathetic, rigid individuals who, regardless of their class origins, neither identify with nor related well to their working-class African-American pupils" (Foster, 1990, p. 123).

In her pioneering research on black K-12 public school teachers, Michele Foster (1990, 1991, 1993, 1997) studied "exemplary" teachers throughout the country—New England, the South, the Midwest, and the West Coast—who taught in segregated and desegregated schools. Foster's work has been used to describe "culturally relevant teaching" or the idea that teachers should possess black cultural knowledge about the students they teach to support academic achievement, cultural competence, and a sociopolitical consciousness (Ladson-Billings, 1995). The implicit assumption here is that black cultural knowledge necessarily translates into successful teaching of all black children in public schools. In Foster's account, race receives vastly more weight than class or gender. For example, Foster (1993) neglects the class distinctions she herself notes, because they have the potential to pose problems to a harmonious racial and cultural discourse:

> It is my contention that the teachers who participated in my study are successful because they are proficient in community norms—that is, they are able to communicate with students in a familiar cultural idiom. Moreover, their success is also due to their understanding of the current as well as the historical, social, economic, and political relationships of their community to the larger society. These teachers are not merely educating the mind—*they are educating for character, personal fulfillment and success in the larger society as well as for competence in the local community.*" (p. 391) (Emphasis mine)

Although Foster acknowledges that black teachers before integration possessed cultural knowledge and political clarity (Beauboeuf-Lafontant, 1999), she overlooks the very nature and substance of their knowledge and "politics." Still, the question remains: What was the nature and substance of Jim Crow's teachers' politics in classrooms and schools? This chapter addresses how the politics of respectability (as a discourse and a logic system) shaped teachers' ideas about "character, personal fulfillment, and success" within and outside of the black community.

The outstanding work of Vanessa Siddle Walker (1996a, 1996b, 2000, 2001, 2005) has provided much of what we know about the history of black teachers in the South before integration.[2] In her groundbreaking book, *Their Highest Potential*, a historical ethnography of the school she attended, Siddle Walker (1996) focused "primarily on the school environment that was created for teaching and learning during segregation" (p. 11). She searched for "interviewees who would have a range of relationships to the school, including students who completed high school and those who didn't, parents who lived varying distances from the school and students who were involved in numerous school activities and those who were not" (p. 222). As an educational historian, Siddle Walker's work also benefits from archival materials combined with interviews as "a solution to the inevitable influence of nostalgia" (p. 223).

Arguably the lead architect in the reconstruction of a history and memory of legally segregated schools for blacks, Siddle Walker (2001) has sought to expose the contradictory images of black teachers. As Siddle Walker stated, "Although [black teachers] worked in constrained educational circumstances, they were not debilitated by these circumstances. Rather teachers were increasingly well-trained educators who worked in concert with their leaders to implement a collective vision of how to educate African American children in a Jim Crow society" (p. 753). Again, what was the political nature and substance of this "collective vision" and how did it shape the perspectives and actions of black teachers before integration? In this chapter, I extend Michele Foster and Vanessa Siddle Walker's work. Did all teachers espouse the same philosophies of educating black children? If not, what were these philosophies and how were they practiced in schools? Did all teachers see themselves in their students? What might have hindered teachers from working toward the advancement of all students? With these questions in mind, I explore how the politics of respectability shaped the nature of black teachers' perceptions and actions in the all-black school before integration.

WHAT "RESPECTABLE" TEACHERS OUGHT TO BE AND TO DO

Drawing upon oral interview data that I collected in Edgecombe, Wilson, and Nash counties in the coastal plain of North Carolina, I used the constant comparative method (Strauss and Corbin, 1998) to extend three of five general themes that Siddle Walker (2001) identified in a historiography of African American teaching between 1940 and 1960. Because there was already existing theory about teaching and learning before integration, I employed extant categories—relating the curriculum, caring about students, and maintaining relationships with community. I then asked new questions to the data about class differences in order to extend and to build upon existing theory (Strauss and Corbin, 1998). Setting out to extend Michele Foster (1997) and Siddle Walker's (1996) work, I initially used questions from their published interview schedules as models with a particular focus on what it was like to teach in all-black schools before integration.

My analytical approach in this multiple site study differs from single site studies, such as Siddle Walker (1996), in two important ways. First, I am able to explore "multiple settings" to "enhance generalizability" (Huberman & Miles, 1994, p. 435). Second, my research data point to thematic collective remembering across schools and communities, and thus help address criticisms that previous findings in one school or community are anecdotal and limited to a specific setting. I analyzed interviews to locate examples from the data that both confirmed and disconfirmed three general principles: 1. Teachers should relate the curriculum to students' needs; 2. Teachers should care about students; 3. Teachers should develop a relationship with the community.

RELATING THE CURRICULUM TO STUDENTS' NEEDS

Expectations for black child labor in the southern agricultural economy led black teachers to go around–or jump across–educational barriers. In rural North Carolina, as I discussed in Chapter 2, poor and working class black children worked the cotton and tobacco fields alongside their parents (Rodgers, 1975). According to participants, students who stayed out of school to work did so for at least two reasons: 1.) White landowners demanded that black sharecroppers and tenant farmers keep their children away from schools, and 2.) Poor and working-class families usually depended upon the wages that children earned.[3] Participants also recalled that some students missed more than a month of school to "pick cotton" or "barn tobacco." Catherine Taylor remembered, "At the first of the year, our kids would be out so much that we just combined our classes. . . . But we were doing what educators today call team-teaching. We did it out of necessity. . . . Again, this is a case of working with the children. If they were not there, you just had to bring them up when they came back. As I said, so many would be out because they were picking tobacco or picking cotton, then we would combine [classes]. We just worked with the children, that's all to it." Although the allotment of money on average daily attendance was a major disadvantage for the rural all-black school, teachers worked with what they had to circumvent the impact of seasonal agricultural work on curriculum and instruction (Rodgers, 1975, p. 45).

Participants guided and motivated students across curricula barriers and blind spots by making the curriculum relate to students' lives. For example, Josephine Edwards explained how she made aspects of the state-mandated science curriculum relevant to the lives of her rural students:

> I was teaching science over here at Darden [School]. To [explain to] the children which is heavier water or oil, do you know what my experiment was? [I'd ask] 'When your mama boils a pot of collards, what's on the top of that water?' They would say, 'the grease that mama skims off.' You know about that, don't you? That's how we had to improvise. They didn't know about the ocean–a barge breaks loose and there's an oil spill. But, they did know about mama boiling that pot of collards and that grease on the top. How did our children get to where they are? Black teachers improvised.

Teaching rural black children required teachers to think about geographical, as well as racial, disadvantages that they often encountered in textbooks. In the Age of Jim Crow, black teachers "generally came from the community in which they taught or from similar African American communities [and] as a result, the teachers brought to the classroom a good deal of understanding about the needs of the students" (Siddle Walker, 2004, p. 80). As Ladson-Billings (2000) noted, "students' own knowledge form[ed] the basis of inquiry either as part of the official curriculum or as it interact[ed] with the official curriculum" (p. 210). Jeffries (1994) has argued that such improvisational or trickster acts in the classroom were the norm among black teachers. Clearly, Edwards's efforts to relate the curriculum to students' needs derive from an understanding of and embeddedness in black rural culture.

Besides a common culture and racial identity, the geopolitical realities of the rural South shaped black teacher' work. Teachers had to adapt and adjust to deeply racist farming communities in which they worked (Anderson, 1988; Litwack, 1998). Among some teachers I interviewed "flexible grouping" became a common classroom practice to deal with an agrarian population depended upon child labor in the first one or two months of school. Like Catherine Taylor who combined classes at the high school level, some elementary teachers remarked:

> I had to do a lot of grouping. Those students who had been coming I could put in one group and then I could move on. Those who had not been, I had to put them into another group and teach. Now they would not stay out two or three days. If it took two weeks or three weeks to get that cotton picked, they stayed out. So, you had to go back and re-teach a lot.
>
> (Fannie Coston)

> We grouped the children. I always had groups. I had groups A, B, and C or 1, 2, and 3. Some children were moving forward faster and they had to work together. It was like group work everyday. You hardly had anything that you taught the whole class. . . . We tried to teach them on a level where they were.
>
> (Helen Toney)

In another account, however, Athalene Emory explained that her school did not use grouping but they did believe strongly in "working with the children." Emory stated:

> We did not group our students. . . . Our philosophy was—from the time we left college—you teach the child where you find them. . . . If you are building a house, you can't begin on the second floor unless you have gotten the foundation done. Therefore, this is the same kind of feelings that we had in regards to our students.

The focus here is less on whether or not teachers used "flexible grouping," but more on the philosophy behind their chosen method. Each participant told stories about teaching children "where you find them" that revealed a broader vision of uplift.

Teachers were rooted in black culture and communities, but their pedagogical actions were grounded in social and political commitments. Under the power-laden circumstances in which teachers taught, Frazier's indictment of black teachers seems unfair. Remember that Frazier (1957) argued that black teachers as members of the middle class showed "no interest in the 'liberation' of Negroes except as it affected their own status" (p. 235). In the three counties I studied, participants were certainly considered members of the middle class as "schoolteachers." Contrary to Frazier, in their collective remembering, participants expressed a collective social aspiration and commitment to move students off the "white man's farm," literally and figuratively.

Every participant emphasized that they worked with parents to provide an education that would uplift both students and families. For example, Arcenia Hines recalled:

> We had to visit every parent at the beginning of the year before we met with the children—not to see what kind of home they had but to see the living conditions—then you would know better about how to work with that child.

In another example, Pauline White stated:

> Sometimes you had parents that were very eager for their children not to come up the way they came up. So, they would say: "I hate to ask you, but are you gon' be too busy on Saturday that you might could come by my home." . . . To us, it was a visitation to make sure that this race did not come up the way that we had found them to be.

But it was not "race" alone that motivated teachers. As members of the race who had "made it," teachers saw it as their responsibility to help pull poor and working-class families out of their economic situations through education. Pedagogical acts, such as home visits and home tutoring, reinforced often unspoken commitments to mutual progress rooted in the politics of respectability.

Unlike Arcenia Hines and Pauline White, who remembered that teachers were required to make home visits, there were others who recalled being encouraged with no formal rule to do so. For example, Equiller Lucas explained that the area where she taught was so spread out and depressed that she did not spend much time traveling around to students' homes. In her interview, Lucas recalled:

Lucas: I did some home visits—very few! [laughter] Well, under the circumstances, I just didn't bother to go into a lot of the homes. After you spend your 7 or 8 hours at school, you didn't have much energy left to do a lot of home visiting.
Kelly: Was it required?
Lucas: No, it wasn't required. We did a lot of writing notes home and that was about it. In the situation I worked in, they did not have telephones and they were using outhouses. They didn't have transportation.

While there were only a few teachers who actually remember "home visits" as a formal rule, most teachers talked about it as the respectable thing to do as a teacher in the community. These findings about home visits as an expectation for classroom teachers are consistent with other studies (Siddle Walker, 1996; Noblit and Dempsey, 1996; Foster, 1997; Philipsen, 1999). Catherine Hines recalled that her principal required them to not only make home visits but also attend church services regularly throughout the county. Whether they were required or not, home visits relieved possible class antagonisms once teachers were able to see the situations and circumstances in which their students lived.

Contrary to Frazier's claim that black teachers' primary concern was "teaching as a source of income," the North Carolina teachers I interviewed reported that they often supplemented, facilitated, and subsidized the curricula so that students did not suffer because of poor and outdated resources. Anniebelle Ricks remembers driving around town asking farmers in the county for small amounts of tobacco to give to her father to sell in order to purchase classroom materials and supplies. Helen Toney remembers buying most of the supplies that her students used in the first grade because parents could not afford "big pencils" [age appropriate] and skill-building workbooks. Cleveland Lewis and Hazel Lewis talked heatedly about a "teacher tax" which their black principals demanded that teachers pay at the beginning of the school year to help defray the cost for basic materials and supplies. Josephine Edwards recalled that her principal bullied the faculty into purchasing a piano for school programs. Almost all the teachers I interviewed had dreaded memories about "mandatory" fundraisers in which teachers were required to raise a certain amount of money each year to offset the under-funding of their schools. When you consider these hidden transcripts, black teachers were a major source of revenue—basically subsidizing the curricula—in a collective (sometimes coercive) struggle for advancement.

Collective remembering among the black teachers I interviewed uncovers hidden transcripts which support the idea that legally segregated schools for blacks were not without resources, albeit resource deprived. Hidden transcripts illustrate how teachers and administrators met the needs of teachers and students in creative ways, fostering strong ties between teachers, students, and families. Still, Frazier's charge raises an important question: How did class differences between teachers and students shape teaching and learning in the all-black school before integration? Nearly all of the teachers that I interviewed were first-generation college students who were raised on farms or in rural communities very much like the students they taught (Siddle Walker, 2000). For example, participants echoed feelings of interconnectedness which shaped their teaching:

> [We] had lived segregation. We lived that life under segregation. Therefore, we knew. We passed those experiences onto the students, so they could better themselves and, not only that, be prepared for the workforce."
>
> (James Buchanan)

> All of the families went to the same churches and the same schools, so they were hearing the same messages all of the time. Everybody was talking about what you can be, what you will do, what I expect of you, what I expect of your behavior. So, they were hearing uplifting messages all of the time.
>
> (Gloria Gray)

While the black elite and middle class in urban centers, such as Washington, D.C. or Chicago, may have been a class of and for itself, as Frazier argued, the teachers I interviewed were new arrivals to the black middle class. These teachers perceived education as a tool for uplifting the race and themselves as active agents in cultivating a positive black identity for poor and working class youth.

Rather than limiting teachers' actions to "gaining status" and "teaching morals and manners," respectability shaped their sense of purpose and gave them hope. As the first to move up and beyond the conditions of their parents, participants in my study expressed a desire to teach their own that overshadowed class antagonisms. For example, Alton Bobbitt remarked:

> When I went to Frederick Douglass [High School] back in the early 1960s, we were using textbooks that were ten years old. . . . It wasn't a

fair proposition, but it was something that we had to deal with. Many teachers who had gone to graduate school in Pennsylvania, New York—you see we could not go to graduate school [in white universities in North Carolina]. The state [of North Carolina] would pay you to go out of state, so there were teachers who went out to Kansas, Penn State, NYU, and City College. Many teachers brought back a repertoire of materials that was up-to-date, that was modern, and luckily we had a [duplicating] machine.[4]

Like Alton Bobbitt, Josephine Edwards also recalled: "Many of us bought materials and books. [White businesses] got rich off black teachers going up there and buying materials to supplement what you had in your classroom—because you had nothing. . . . You [would] see material that read 'not to be [copied].' You couldn't run it off like it [was] because it said 'not to be copied,' so you had to rephrase some of it in order to [use] it." It was both the "place" (the South) and the "times" (Age of Jim Crow) which shaped black teachers' work and discourse. In their collective remembering, black teachers uncovered a responsibility to serve those less fortunate within the race.

CARING ABOUT POOR AND WORKING-CLASS BLACK STUDENTS

Working against a societal myth of black inferiority, black teachers cared about their poor and working-class students. As Siddle Walker (2004) explained, "caring had a purpose . . . To care intensely for the students for whom they had been given responsibility was to provide them with a storehouse of tools for challenging and thwarting a deeply imbedded system of inequality" (91). Contrary to accounts of uncaring and undedicated teachers (see critique by Foster, 1990), participants in my study confirmed claims that "caring" was an essential ingredient to the "good" segregated school:

> I think the first thing that you would write about black teachers before integration is that they cared about their children. They taught them, yes, but they cared about the children and that is where all the good teaching came from.
>
> (Catherine Taylor)

> [Black students] had someone who could look at [them] and know what they actually needed. When I say what they actually needed, they needed more than just education: we talked about our health, character . . . self-respect first and then how to respect others. I can look now and see students, everywhere, who know that I was concerned about their education, their character, their self-esteem—the whole person.
>
> (Effie Smith)

In these accounts, analyses of race and culture do not explain everything. Participants possessed an uplift ideology that permeated class distinctions and pledged to ameliorate class situations. They wished and hoped for better lives for all of their students. As "role models," a term that Effie Smith later used in her interview, upwardly mobile and middle class black teachers taught rural children lessons in "health, character, self-respect, and respect for others" as a strike against white supremacist notions of black immorality and inferiority. While "race" was certainly a factor, participants were concerned about students' class location and family situations. Drawing upon familiar clichés, these black teachers had "made it" or "beat the odds." In their positions as college-educated teachers, they worked to make sure that others sought and achieved respectability through middle-class lifestyles.

There is a breakdown in the counter-narrative about "caring" in legally segregated schools for blacks, however. While teachers worked toward collective social aspirations and advancement for all students, caring in the everyday often coexisted with class production and reproduction processes in subtle ways. Despite their best efforts, participants acknowledged that not every individual would make it. Ultimately, students themselves would have to decide whether or not they wanted to reach beyond their rural, poor, and working class circumstances. While teachers possessed the knowledge and awareness that students needed, they believed that individuals had to want it for themselves:

> The goal was to help that student make a livelihood in life. Now that depended upon what that student wanted to do. You could tell just about if the student was going to end up in the technical field or whether that student was going to go on to college—basically by the way he or she carried themselves and how well they paid attention in the classroom.
> (James Buchanan)

> I enjoyed it [teaching] because we bonded together ... kids can tell when they're loved. We were special together. I would share my experiences with those students because I would say, "you don't have to make excuses because we are black ... If you don't have anything now, it's okay. It is not your fault. If you have a home where you don't even have steps, it is not your fault. But don't let me catch you ten years from now [without steps]. (You know, these were high school juniors and seniors.) I am going to blame you. I've even had students come back for reunions and say, 'hey Mrs. Hunter, I don't jump in my house anymore.' They [were] trying to say that there is something I said that made a difference.
> (Nellie Hunter)

These accounts support Monica White's (2004) assertion that "black teachers at that time felt a moral obligation to prepare each student for success in facing the challenges of discrimination in a racially segregated world" (p. 150). Although the goal may have been universal and collective, the politics of respectability required each individual to make a choice. In each of the narratives above, "bourgeois respectability" pervaded participants' narratives: James Buchanan's judgments about who could or would succeed and Nellie Hunter's informal classroom talks about respectable homes.

Some participants talked about teachers who used a "theoretical" white boy or white girl to discipline and to motivate black children to achieve. According to Gaines (1996), "the problem with racial uplift ideology is thus one of unconscious internalized racism" (p. 6). Although I understand claims that using white people as "the standard" is an indicator of "internalized racism," I also want to offer an alternative explanation that takes in consideration how "being respectable" sometimes required the use of imaginary or theoretical whites to produce results. Doretha Jones recalled that when she was in school in the 1940s and 1950s, black teachers in her school often reprimanded students by saying, "white students would not leave paper on the floor," "white children would never do this," or "white children would never do that." Consequently, Doretha Jones explained that when she became a teacher she said many of these same things to her students. She remembered: "They taught us, 'you got to learn this material because you are behind.' Everywhere we went, they would say 'you are behind.' But they didn't know whether or not we were behind, because we didn't know what the [white] people were doing. Then, when we started teaching, we were saying the same things." In contrast, Lucille Edwards recalled: "When I taught, regardless of the children, I never taught that we were behind. My thinking was that since we are on a different socioeconomic level and when we go into the job market, we have to be a bit better." Without a doubt, the participants in my study cared about the life circumstances of the rural black children they taught. Rather than internalized racism, I read the hidden transcripts as a message to black youth about whites as competition—not superior.

Whether we approve or disapprove of their verbal reprimands, many black teachers—like most Americans at this time—subscribed to the belief that upward mobility was a contest or a game. Inferring from interview data, however, my participants viewed the contest as an unfair competition between blacks and whites. In his interview, Henry Davis described this kind of caring as "tough love" which was common among black teachers. Participants wanted to push students out of their old ways and demand that they strive:

> But we were trying to teach them the things they were going to have to come up against and what they were going to have to experience. For example, we had to teach the black child that he had to be just a little bit better to get the same type of job that the white child got.
>
> (E.J. Cummings)

> We could work close to kids—there was just camaraderie you know—and if I wanted to talk to you and tell you something . . . [I could] because being black myself I could come up and sit with you and tell you: 'the only thing that is going to prepare you is an education, so get your act together now.'
>
> (Henry Davis)

> I think that we were so [pause] trying to make our children [pause] wake them up. You know, this is a new day, you have to take off and do something. We tried to get them to study more, do more, you know, excel [pause] as much as you can. You see we could talk to them because it was a situation in which there were no white people there and you could motivate those children to get going. [pause] I mean that's something that I remember doing a lot—trying to get them to the place that they could go beyond the four year school—beyond the high school, you know, because some of them were a little complacent. They just didn't want to do anything beyond high school other than go get a job.
>
> (Carol Cooper)

Oral interviews support Siddle Walker's (2001) assertion that "at the root of [black teachers'] practices was the commonly held belief that Blacks had to be taught to be better than White students if they were to succeed" (p. 769).

Sociologist Ralph Turner (1986) has speculated that the "accepted mode of upward mobility" actually shapes schooling practices. In other words, it is understandable that some black teachers, like coaches in a game, might try to arouse their players through psychological interventions, such that the other team is used to motivate and to stimulate their players. As a common norm about upward mobility, black teachers were not only conscious of how white supremacy was a constant threat against black social mobility, but also they thought it was necessary to raise a team that could beat the "white man" at his own game—not to mention that it was the only game in town.

There was a "politics" of caring that had just as much to do with the geopolitics of race and racism as a common racial identity. In the face of state-sponsored racial discrimination, participants motivated, pushed, and challenged black students to excel. Samuel Gray reflected:

> Although you knew about the limitations, you were still pushing students to become doctors, engineers, and attorneys—knowing that they would not be able to get a job. But the main thing [was] that it would prepare more people who looked like you who would not accept what the system was putting on you.
>
> (Samuel Gray)

In order to make my point, I continue with a story told by Gray about the year he discovered that the black high school had to pay the white high school in order to play their team sports in the "public" park. As a prominent coach in the county, Gray complained often—loudly and publicly—until the black principal asked him to cease his protest. Gray remembered:

> He asked me not to go over there [to the white high school]. And these were his words: 'I am afraid of white folks.' If he had not told me the truth, I would have dealt with it totally. But when he was so honest [pause] black men his age, and my father's age, didn't have the courage that we had. And he said to me, and I had just gotten out of the military, I was 25, he said, 'it's going to take young men like you to change things.'

Gray explained that he respected his principal's wishes, but he continued to talk to students and parents about the injustice. Gray explained, "Our kids needed to be motivated and inspired, but they also needed to know the truth about the system—one black and one white—that existed in this country. And, I found myself talking about it quite often." White supremacy permeated black and white society but it was challenged by some black teachers daily in all-black schools. Although Gray was limited by what he could do in the public view, he turned his classroom into a site of resistance by having honest conversations "behind the scenes" about racism with his students.

Further research should explore how youth in all-black schools actually experienced their teachers and their pedagogic interventions and strategies. I have as yet made no systematic effort to find out how students understood and interpreted the words and sentiments of their teachers. Rodgers (1975) surveyed thirty students who had graduated from all-black high schools between 1962 and 1973, but the only information that he reports is how they felt about integration.[5] Since participants were also former students of all-black schools, I have been able to gather a few anecdotes that give us some clues about possible negative experiences and feelings. Doretha Jones stated that she refused to submit an application to teach in the county where she graduated because she did not want to work with the "mean" teachers who taught her. Other teachers, such as Roosevelt Pitt, Nellie Hunter, and Josephine Edwards, reflected upon how incredibly "strict" and "dogmatic" their teachers and principals were about their speech, attitude, and behavior.

Nearly all of the teachers that I interviewed said that, in hindsight, they understood the messages that their teachers tried to communicate. They also believed that for many students the message was clouded by the harsh manner in which it could be delivered. Most teachers in my study remembered their teachers fondly and gave them a great deal of credit for their decision to go to college. In sum, the politics of respectability shaped caring in schools. Respectability became the justification for why teachers cared and why they were so hard on students; they were simply trying to uplift the race in a world of injustice and inequality.

DEVELOPING A "RESPECTABLE" RELATIONSHIP WITH THE COMMUNITY

Across three counties, black communities held the teaching profession and their teachers in high regard. Teaching was a "respectable" occupation for young men and women. As a former student of an all-black school and the second black woman to earn a Ph.D. in mathematics, Evelyn Boyd Granville described the importance of black teachers to black communities: "And, of course, our greatest, our most evident role models then were black, colored, Negro teachers. And of course, the teachers represented success; they represented stability in the community. They lived better than anybody else, and so naturally, you wanted to be like they were. And in order to be like they were, you needed an education" (Murray, 2001, p. 64). All participants agreed that before integration black teachers sat on a pedestal in the black community—whether they wanted to sit on it or not.

In her interview, Nellie Hunter discussed an unspoken tension between black teachers and the black community. Though she did not state it explicitly, presuming that I might have already known, Hunter mentioned that some people in the black community thought that black teachers were "bourgeois" (used as a derogatory word in the black community which referred to a member of the black elite or middle class who thought that they were a "better class of blacks"). Hunter reflected:

> I never thought that I had arrived. Other people may have thought that we were better than the rest.... Somebody would say 'you're a teacher' and I would say 'you're a teacher, too.' One philosopher said every man is my superior because I may learn from him. And if you can play the piano, you are my superior. I can learn from you.

It is reasonable that some college-educated black teachers in the Age of Jim Crow did think that they were "better than the rest;" however, participants in my study remembered a strong, emotional, and connected relationship to the communities in which they lived and worked.

As I discussed earlier, participants reported that they worked with parents and the entire community through home visits, school programs, and community events. A common theme in the literature on black teachers is the strong and healthy relationships that community members had before integration (Franklin, 1990; Foster, 1997; Noblit and Dempsey, 1996; Siddle Walker, 1996a). Similarly, participants had fond memories of parents:

> You had parents who could not read a lick, but their kids are now doctors and lawyers because they had a desire for their kids to get places and to perform. So, I think that is one of the basic things that we can't forget—the desire [that parents had] for their kids to learn, to perform, and to make their place in life.
>
> (Joseph Ray)

> The teacher could do no wrong and the students knew it. As a result, you didn't have any [discipline] problems—not that many kids caused a problem. The parents were with you at the PTA (Parent Teacher Association).... Parents came out to see their children perform [during holiday programs] and they were encouraging their children.
>
> (Vera Tyson)

Participants suggested that parents played a supportive role and treated teachers with a great deal of respect.

Teachers worked to uplift communities for the betterment and advancement of both children and families (Foster, 1990, 1991; Noblit and Dempsey, 1996; Siddle Walker, 1996, 2004) but they had to abide by written and unwritten rules about what it meant to be a respectable teacher:

> You had to be involved in the entire community. If you lived in a community, you had to visit the various churches and put yourself in their social events. You had to be involved more in the community than you did with [school] integration. With integration, we went to school, we taught, [and] we left. But, in the black schools, you didn't.
>
> (Jessie Jones)

> You had to walk a chalk line.... One of the requirements was that if a person was out of town that person had to set up residence in that town for at least one year. I was in Rocky Mount, but I had to move. I moved to a church member's house. I had to live there in Spring Hope.
>
> (Annie Beasley)

> We didn't wear anything that we wanted to. In fact, I started teaching in 1963. It was illegal for [women] teachers to wear pants. Well, I know at the black school; I can't tell you about the others. [Women] had to wear stockings. We had to be well-dressed like we were taught in college. There was a dress code for teachers.
>
> (Doretha Jones)

Many teachers stayed in the teaching profession because they were connected to a community in which they were expected to nurture and to serve.

Long-term employment patterns and long-term community residence were common for the majority of the teachers I interviewed, which has been documented in other studies (Foster, 1991; Siddle Walker, 1996b). Many highly-educated black teachers could have left the K-12 classroom for careers at the college-level or sought employment in government jobs through civil service tests.[6] However, my participants continued to work in all-black schools in North Carolina—even those teachers who never married, earned an advanced degree, and might have gone elsewhere. For example, Jessie Jones and Annie Beasley graduated from Shaw University and started non-teaching careers in New York as a research assistant in a chemical lab and as a government civil servant, respectively. Both left "good" jobs in New York in less than two years after college to begin careers in teaching. Both had taken some education classes in college, but they sought teaching positions because it was a respectable job for college-educated blacks with few opportunities in rural areas. Neither married but had strong obligations and commitments to family and to church. Both received master's degrees before integration and both retired from integrated public schools in the early 1990s. When I asked each of them why she stayed in the teaching profession, considering each had begun careers in the North, they both talked about a commitment to teaching and helping black children, as well as a genuine love of teaching. They recalled the "good times" they had in all-black schools and communities, describing a vibrant intellectual school culture and a supportive family-like school community that sustained them. Many teachers, like Jessie Jones and Annie Beasley, made important connections between their own skills, knowledge, and credentials with student learning (or not learning) in all-black schools. The lives and careers of black teachers became a living testimony for racial uplift among rural black youth for generations.

A common metaphor in the literature on the "good" segregated school is the idea that the all-black school was like a family. Nearly all of the participants in my study described the all-black school and community in this way:

> So there was a lot of togetherness and it was more like a family. I felt like I was an extension of their [real] family. Because whenever they were sick, we would take the lessons to them. And, teach them at home without additional pay.
>
> (Jessie Jones)

> Well I think it is the same kind of strategies that you use with your own family if you have children. You have children on different levels—you don't categorize them. You come to the table and everybody learns from everybody else.
>
> (Athalene Emory)

However, some participants' accounts revealed a breakdown in the family metaphor. For instance, Josephine Edwards recalled tension among teachers:

> We had cooperation of course [pause] envy—we had some envy there. [Kelly: What do you mean by envy?] Well, I went to Darden [School]. I was young and I had a master's degree [from Pennsylvania State University] . . . I am one like this: if you are jealous of me, then you have the problem. And I just kept right on going and to this day, if somebody is envious of me, they have the problem. I'm a Nash County kind of girl and I shall never forget my roots out of Nash County where I picked cotton and tobacco and I did all of it. But envy, you know, if you do something and do it well, you know, people are envious of you.

Another example came from Nellie Hunter, who stated that there was class tension between some teachers and students:

> My worst memories prior to integration [were] that there were a lot of ill things said to children. . . . I had a student tell me, which could have been the same thing with me but it just happened to be her day, that a teacher told her: 'you ain't nothing and you never will be.' . . . And there was a preconceived notion that you can't get the A. Some [teachers] would say: 'The author has the A because he wrote the book, the teacher gets the B because I am teaching it, and the best you can get is a C." Have you ever heard that expression? Well, it was said during those years. The girl who told me this came out of a 9 or 10 person family like I did. 'The best you can get is a C' and a lot of times students might have been super brilliant. She was told that 'you won't be anything" because she had come from a family like I did.

In this particular case, some teachers drew upon bourgeois respectability, discriminating against children who came from the wrong side of the tracks or who were raised in large families—especially if there was no father around. Gloria Burks also recalled that skin color differences challenged the notion that the all-black school was one big happy family:

> If you were light [skinned], then you were a favorite; and if you had nice hair, then you were a favorite. Even in the band, you couldn't be a majorette unless you had a *little* color to you and [long] pretty hair—it wasn't who could do it the best. It was what you looked like.

Clearly, the culture of respectability had serious implications for the various kinds of relationships that teachers might have developed in all-black school communities.

Alongside their feelings of responsibility and missionary spirit, interviews brought out latent reports of "ill things" said and done to poor and working class students in the name of racial uplift. These data indicate that some "respectable" teachers were not able to completely surpass class-related ideological barriers at the same time that they motivated students to exceed racist societal expectations. From a student's point of view, Sylvia Jones (2006) confirmed, "teachers also represented the professional class, and in my experience, treated students who were more like them, or in the same social circle as their parents, with more tolerance, care, and concern" (p. 301). Ultimately, however, the politics of respectability compels us to reconsider how we use "family" as a metaphor to talk about "good" segregated schools, teachers, and communities before integration.

THE GEOPOLITICS OF RACE AND CLASS

These findings confirm Michelle Foster and Vanessa Siddle Walker's point that black teachers were rooted in black culture and community, which aided their teaching in the Age of Jim Crow. As hidden transcripts suggest, the politics of respectability shaped black teachers' work in the coastal plain of North Carolina. The geopolitics of race and racism in rural North Carolina compelled teachers to adopt a broader vision of uplift for both racial and class justice. Black teachers adapted and adjusted their teaching practices to meet the curricular needs of their students. Teachers cared about their students as they worked against a societal myth of black inferiority. In a time of state-sponsored racial discrimination and segregation, the social situation demanded a "politics" for racial uplift and mutual progress. Teachers also developed a respectable relationship with the community which meant that they were expected to serve students and families. In this role, teachers were held in high regard and placed on a proverbial pedestal with written and unwritten rules about what a teacher should do (e.g., home visits) and should not do (e.g., live outside the community).

One participant, Athalene Emory, stated at the end of her interview that black teachers "were golden nuggets that most people didn't know about." Throughout my analysis, I have referred to two metaphors—the coach and the family—that I believe capture important aspects of black teachers before integration. Briefly, I return to these two metaphors to depict the relationship that I see between black teachers and the politics of respectability. In the first metaphor, black teachers indeed were like coaches who worked with players, individually and collectively, so that the team could win games. Sometimes the opposing team was used to motivate players to work harder, but the coach cared for the team and showed an interest in winning games. Thinking back to Frazier's claim about black teachers, as well as counter-narratives of the "good" segregated school and its teachers, scholars have been debating the very nature of Jim Crow's teachers—their perceptions and actions. As I stated earlier, the first position argued that black teachers considered themselves as a "better class," while the second position implied that black teachers were a "race with no class." As a third position, I argue that when you consider that the black teachers I studied were deeply concerned with the realities of living in a Jim Crow society, it makes sense that they recognized the importance of racial and class uplift in their students' lives. We can see race and class in teachers' accounts by exploring the politics of respectability in black teachers' perceptions and actions.

In the second metaphor, participants who are long-term residents and workers relate to their all-black school communities as a family. (Most of the teachers I interviewed had taught three or four generations of students from the same family.) Initially when I heard participants report "ill things" that were said and done to students and teachers, I questioned whether the family metaphor actually explained how things really were before integration. Eventually, I thought about my own family which is made up of different people with different genders, different talents, and different personalities. As individuals within a collective, we do not always get along but that does not mean that we are not a family. Therefore, stories of envy, jealousy, and sometimes rage that participants uncovered in their interviews do not destroy the idea that the all-black school was "like a family." Rather these stories push the literature on "good" or "valued" segregated schools toward (re)presenting them in the way they really were. Using the politics of respectability as a theoretical lens enables us to ask new critical questions about "conflict and disorder" alongside "cooperation and order."

Further research could explore a host of questions, such as: In the "good" segregated school, how did class differences among black children lead to different outcomes in schooling and life? What were the formal and informal mechanisms employed by black teachers before integration to encourage poor and working-class students to go to college? These questions and others require us to think through problems that black teachers faced before integration that could inform contemporary problems in education. Ultimately, there needs to be a disruption in counter-narratives of the "good" and "valued" segregated school and its teachers as always functional, egalitarian, and successful.

In a final response to Frazier, hidden transcripts drew my attention to a changing respectability discourse after the Great Depression which might explain why black teachers in my study had social and political commitments to civil rights and social power. Through flexible grouping, home visits, purchasing material and supplies, and supplementing the curriculum through graduate course work, teachers were, as Pauline White stated, "[making] sure that this race did not come up the way that [they] had found them to be." Black teachers had a broader vision of racial uplift that encouraged and motivated rural poor and working-class students to "move off the farm" and into middle-class lifestyles. It would be a mistake to suggest, as Frazier did, that black teachers linked themselves entirely to "bourgeois respectability"—seeking status and acceptance from whites through image and reputation. I have shown that participants talked to their students about the immorality and injustice of white racism at the same time that they worked on reforming individual behavior (character, self-esteem, and speech) in their classrooms. Some teachers worked to dispel the myth of black inferiority using a "theoretical white" as the target goal for black students to not only reach but to surpass.

Far from uncaring, self-serving, and status-addicted teachers, participants in my study worked together in a collective struggle to improve the socioeconomic status of rural black children in the South. Instead of limiting or constraining black teachers' work, the politics of respectability actually gave them a sense of purpose and hope to forge ahead. There are clear cases in which the message of uplift may have gotten lost in some teachers' promotion and enactment of "tough love." From the teacher's point of view, however, some students were "complacent" and needed to be "awakened" "motivated," "pushed," and "inspired." Under what conditions, then, might teachers have employed a broader vision of uplift through respectability? The answer, I believe, does not lie within an analysis of "culture and community" alone. Southern black teachers thought about teaching as a geopolitical practice for respectability with the hope of jobs, rights, and social power for tomorrow's black children. "Facing the same opponent of white supremacy," as historian Leslie Brown (2008) aptly pointed out, "the shared struggle counted more . . . than fragile differences" (p. 38).

5 A Strategy of Opportunity
Black Teachers and the Making of a New Form of Capital

In the Age of Jim Crow, black teachers were a major resource for black achievement and social mobility (Fairclough, 2007; Shircliffe, 2006; Siddle Walker, 1996). Black teachers fashioned situated pedagogies for the acquisition of skills, knowledge, and credentials that could be used in exchange for jobs, rights, and social power. To summarize briefly, situated pedagogies refer to teachers "creating responses and initiatives" in classrooms, schools, and communities that have been "shaped by a particular history of oppression and privilege in the lives of their students" (Lather and Ellsworth, 1996, p. 71). Situated pedagogies also consider the social context and the geopolitics of teachers' work (Ladson-Billings, 2000; Lather and Ellsworth, 1996). In the Jim Crow South, the physical and legal segregation of towns, states, and regions loomed large in the responses and initiatives of teachers in classrooms and schools (Delaney, 1998). Consequently, black teachers' work was not disengaged or disconnected from the personal troubles of their black students nor the larger public issues that structured their lives (Mills, 1959).

One of the most troubling issues within the sociology of education, today, has been an overemphasis on cultural explanations of black student underachievement in desegregated school districts, especially those with resource problems (Gould, 1999; Lynn, 2006). Two dominant cultural explanations persist. First, the cultural deficit explanation maintains that some black children suffer from cultural deprivation due to an impoverished family life and negative community forces (See Valentine, 1968; Ogbu, 1981, 1982, 2003). Second, the cultural mismatch explanation claims that black students are academically disengaged and underperform because they are taught by white teachers who do not share their home culture and language (Cross, 2003; Irvine, 1990; Villegas, 1988). In a qualitative study of predominately white pre-service education majors in an elite university, for instance, King and Ladson-Billings (1990) found that their students employed cultural explanations to evaluate problems of black students in school.

This chapter examines teachers' work in legally segregated schools for blacks to look for clues to an enduring intellectual puzzle: how can we educate poor children of color with little resources and unequal funding. Drawing from hidden transcripts in oral interviewing, I introduce and establish a link between the promotion of a new form of "capital" and the educational achievement of black youth during the Jim Crow years. Considering the social and geopolitical predicament of blacks in the Jim Crow South, how did black teachers deal with inequalities and deficits through situated pedagogies? Why might black teachers have understood educational barriers to black achievement and success differently from some educators today? What follows is a detailed explanation of "educational capital" as a new concept to help us think through the puzzle. Ultimately, I show how black teachers promoted the acquisition of educational capital in the form of generating materials and supplies, situating curriculum and instruction, mobilizing human resources, and forging a double consciousness within students.

WHAT IS EDUCATIONAL CAPITAL?

In a translation of Pierre Bourdieu's *Distinction,* Richard Nice used the term "educational capital" to refer to qualifications (academic credentials or certifications) that can be used for social mobility regardless of social origin or family background (Bourdieu, 1984). In consideration of Jim Crow society, not contemporary French society which Bourdieu wrote about in the 1980s, I borrowed and re-imagined the term educational capital to take into account social origin. Educational capital, then, consists of the acquisition of qualifications (i.e., skills, knowledge, and credentials) *through formal schooling* that can be used in exchange for jobs, social power, or other forms of capital. Taking into consideration the geopolitics of the Jim Crow South and the field of the labor market, educational capital was particularly important for subordinate groups in an oppressive society because it was often the only way that they could gain access to opportunities.

Even though Bourdieu's work (1986) on various forms of capital is widely known and applied in sociological and educational research, there has been very little effort to study educational capital as a separate and distinct concept. Bourdieu's notion of capital has three fundamental aspects: economic capital which mainly refers to material resources, like money, income and wealth; social capital which refers to networks of connections that lead to institutional access and desirable positions; and cultural capital which usually refers to high status cultural signals (tastes, preferences, and values) that can lead to social inclusion (Bourdieu 1984, 1986; Lamont and Lareau, 1988, Lareau and Horvat, 1999). In this book, I do not seek to operationalize educational capital. My aim is to introduce the concept for its theoretical possibilities. Future research should explore the specific skills, knowledge, and credentials that black students obtained and map out outcomes before and after integration.

Although Bourdieu gave no clear definition of educational capital as a theoretical concept, I have deduced at least three basic principles in his work. First, educational capital consists of qualifications acquired *through formal schooling*, while cultural capital is understood to be qualifications (e.g., status of being a doctor's child) *acquired first in the home and later developed through schooling*. Second, educational capital carries much weight in certain fields (e.g., education and the labor market) where formal skills, knowledge, and other educational qualifications matter and may not carry any weight in other fields (e.g., home). Third, within an oppressive society, schools can play an important role in the conversion of a subordinate group member's status (from working poor to middle class) in the larger society. In some workplaces and societal positions, however, educational capital may be overlooked because of skin color prejudice and discrimination.

As a new concept, educational capital can be useful for explaining how black teachers in segregated schools prepared and motivated disadvantaged black children to achieve academically and to aspire for occupational and social mobility.[1] However, it requires the reader to be able to disentangle the most familiar forms of capital and to think about them within the context of the Jim Crow South. While my use of the concept is exploratory, educational capital may be generally applicable for other kinds of social and historical analyses. I want to make it clear that black teachers did not promote educational capital *instead of* other forms of capital. Indeed, multiple forms of capital were cultivated and operated.

The promotion of educational capital through situated pedagogies compels us to rethink black teachers' work before integration. In my study, the black teachers I interviewed made conscious decisions to empower students and work against white supremacy. They taught state-mandated curricula but they also sought ways to penetrate the power structure by equipping black youth with educational capital that could be used to access other forms of capital (social, cultural, and economic). In addition to their "traditional" function as cultural bearers, role models, and mentors (Foster, 1990, 1991; Irvine, 1989; Irvine and Hill, 1990; King, 1993; Mitchell, 1998; Siddle Walker, 1996a, 1996b, 2000), I argue that black teachers played a leading and active part in black achievement and social mobility in the United States.

WHAT EDUCATIONAL CAPITAL IS NOT

Educational capital overlaps with and breaks away from other forms of capital, such as human and cultural capital. For example, human capital emphasizes knowledge insofar as it leads to higher earnings and its focus is specifically on economic payoffs (Becker, 1993). Given state-sponsored racism and discrimination, skills and knowledge did not reliably lead to higher incomes. Black teachers' emphasis was not simply on knowledge with an economic payoff; they often emphasized knowledge which could increase racial awareness and pride, as well as knowledge of white racism and discrimination. Consequently, the case of black teachers and teaching in the Jim Crow South presents a unique situation in which the goal of accumulating capital was not only for economic payoff but also for demanding respectability as individuals and as a race.

Distinctively different from educational capital, cultural capital has been defined by some sociologits of education as the acquisition of "high status" cultural signals that can be converted into other forms of capital (DiMaggio, 1982; Kingston, 2001; Lamont and Lareau, 1988). Significantly, Kingston (2001) argued, "cultural capital is not just a general resource available and valuable to everyone; it is largely the property of the existing elite" (p. 89). One way of thinking about high status versus low status is to think about the former as dominant and the latter as subordinate. For example, white, male, and owning characteristics are high status and black, female, and working poor characteristics are low status within the United States socio-historical context. In my analysis, for example, I refer to cultural capital as high status cultural signals (the culture of dominant groups) that can be used to both include and exclude subordinate group members in a world ruled by dominants (Lareau and Horvat, 1999).

Intentionally and unintentionally, after school integration, there was a shift in the intellectual gaze from "social structures" to "cultural capital" to explain black underachievement and failure (Gould, 1999). Within educational studies, the reasoning went like this: black students do not perform well in integrated schools because they lack the cultural capital needed to succeed in those schools. Like "cultural deprivation" and "cultural mismatch," cultural capital has become an explanation of black underachievement and failure in desegregated schools. According to Bennett deMarrais and Lecompte (1999), educators have been led to believe that poor and working-class black parents passed along a cycle of poverty for their future generations because they "attended poor schools, [and] were not adequately prepared for jobs, if and when they finished school" (p. 277). As a consequence, some well-intentioned cultural analyses have unintentionally "blamed the victim" as if the fate of many poor and working-class blacks rested solely upon their individual choices or cultural membership (Gould, 1999).

Recent studies (Carter, 2003, 2005; Franklin & Savage, 2004) have borrowed and extended the concept of cultural capital to include a "nondominant" cultural capital that was acquired and valued in black communities in the Age of Jim Crow. Similarly, my use of educational capital is another effort to counter troubling cultural capital explanations. While cultural capital may have been acquired initially (and primarily) in the home and the larger black community (Carter, 2005), black teachers in all-black schools had the task of uplifting the race beyond the acquisition of cultural capital (e.g., dominant speech, dress, and behavior). Their primary emphasis, I argue, was educational capital that most poor and working-class black parents simply could not give their children. Given the lack of alternatives, educational capital was the accepted mode to social mobility for blacks in a segregated society with state-sponsored racism. Educational capital gave black people hope that formal academic standards or qualifications would be the "great equalizer" despite its limitations in an oppressive society. As the renowned historian John Hope Franklin (2005) remarked: "They could logically and consistently function only if they believed in the educability of everyone and in the power of education to transform the social order" (p. 300).

EDUCATIONAL CAPITAL AND STRATEGIES OF OPPORTUNITY IN BLACK LIFE

At the turn of the 20th century, the leading black scholar, W.E.B. Du Bois (1903/2002) outlined a strategy for the intellectual growth and social mobility of black youth. According to Du Bois, schools should teach "morals and manners incidentally" and should make their primary function "the quickening and training of human intelligence," without replacing "the home as the chief moral teacher" (p. 68). As I have shown in Chapter 3, participants in my study worked with families, churches, and civic organizations to cultivate a cornucopia of tastes, preferences, attitudes, and behaviors from lowbrow to highbrow.[2] As a strategy to widen opportunities for black students, however, the focus on educational capital linked "being respectable" with intelligent work, civil rights and social power. However, Du Bois represented the unpopular voice among black and white subscribers to "industrial education" when he pushed for a greater focus on intelligent work required through higher education.[3]

When Booker T. Washington proclaimed, in his famous 1895 Atlanta Exposition address, that "it is at the bottom of life we must begin, and not at the top" (Mullane, 1993, p. 365), Du Bois responded in his classic essay "The Talented Tenth." Du Bois wrote: "Was there ever a nation on God's fair earth civilized from the bottom upward? Never; it is, ever was, and ever will be from the top downward that culture filters. The Talented Tenth rises and pulls all that are worth the saving up to their vantage ground. This is the history of human progress" (Mullane, 1993, p. 386). Ironically, as Du Bois pointed out, even Booker T. Washington had surrounded himself with college-bred men:

> "Here [Washington] has as helpers the son of a Negro senator, trained in Greeke and the humanities, and graduated at Harvard; the son of a Negro congressman and lawyer, trained in Latin and mathematics, and graduated at Oberlin; he has as his wife, a woman who read Virgil and

Homer in the same class room with me, he has as chaplain, a classical graduate of Atlanta University; as teachers of science, a graduate of Fisk; as teacher of history, a graduate of Smith,—indeed some thirty of his chief teachers are college graduates, and instead of studying French grammars in the midst of weeds, or buying pianos for dirty cabins, they are at Mr. Washington's right hand helping him in a noble work" (Mullane, 1993, 392).

More than an emphasis on "culture" to uplift the race, Du Bois pointed to the quickening and training of intelligence, or what I call the acquisition of educational capital, which Washington himself found essential to have within his reach.

As I define it, educational capital could potentially be converted into other forms of capital (economic, social, and cultural) in both the black community and mainstream white society. The acquisition of educational capital provided certain freedoms for black youth as adults, especially those who wanted to get away from sharecropping or escape menial labor in white-dominated settings. For example, the high school diploma allowed many black youth to move off the farm to earn enough money to help other members of their family. Many black youth enlisted in the armed services, matriculated in a teachers' college or university, or enrolled in trade schools (e.g., beautician and carpentry). Beyond high school, a college education gave students access to better jobs that paid more with fringe benefits which did not come with farm work (economic capital). A good job or college matriculation enhanced a student's social networks, which sometimes led to "government jobs" or moves to the North to start a new life (social capital). In essence, educational capital ensured more than a skill and a credential once it was obtained. Black youth were exposed frequently to situated pedagogies of liberty, freedom, democracy, and civil disobedience that would become a resource in what came to be known as the black civil rights movement (cultural capital).

Through situated pedagogies for the acquisition of educational capital, black teachers sought to lift black youth above the conditions in which they were born and to prepare them for the world of work in a segregated labor market. Scholars should not discount or neglect the daily struggles of black teachers in classrooms and schools as political actors. However, as Lather and Ellsworth (1996) pointed out: "All classroom practices are situated—that is, they take place in institutions, historical moments, cultural and social fields, and in response to individual and social constraints that are often unrepeatable" (p. 70). This chapter, then, considers how a small group of former teachers remembered their classroom practices and teaching experiences in three counties in the coastal plain of North Carolina. Participants drew upon their knowledge of situated pedagogies used in classrooms and schools and of common norms within legally segregated schools and within the black community.

Michele Foster (1990) has argued that "certain societal changes, in particular the dismantling of the 'separate but equal' laws, have created an illusion and convinced many Americans, including a substantial number of younger Blacks [sic], that institutional racism is a thing of the past. [However] the power arrangements have merely been rearranged, not changed" (p. 139). If we take Foster's claims seriously, then an analysis of black teachers' work in all-black schools—which were poorly funded and lacking basic resources like some desegregated schools today—could potentially inform us about what teachers and other educational authorities might do to turn from an analysis of "cultural deficiency" to one of "institutional and structural racism." In my efforts to do so, I raise the following questions: Considering the social, cultural, and economic predicament of poor and rural black children under Jim Crow, how might black teachers have understood educational barriers to black achievement and success? How did black teachers deal with the inequalities and deficits through situated pedagogies? How have cultural capital arguments, for example, moved us away from understanding the success and failure of black students as problems rooted in the continuing significance of race and racism in the United States? Did cultural capital alone explain black students' success or failure?

SITUATED PEDAGOGIES FOR EDUCATIONAL CAPITAL: RESPONSES AND INITIATIVES

The headings in this section have been derived from Lather and Ellsworth's definition of situated pedagogies, but the actual themes emerged from the data. Within these findings, I do not focus on actual student outcomes nor do I provide statistical data about students' acquired educational capital (e.g., the percentage of students who actually graduated from high school and entered higher education). The focus is on teacher responses and initiatives to structural constraints and institutional barriers. As I stated earlier, participants fashioned pedagogies—responses and initiatives shaped by the history and legacy of Jim Crow and the "complexities of the local situation" (Lather and Ellsworth, 1996, p. 71). I will not draw upon one type of situated pedagogy, such as culturally relevant pedagogy (Ladson-Billings, 1995) or politically relevant pedagogy (Beauboeuf-Lafontant, 1999). The formidable task of facilitating the acquisition of educational capital, in rural North Carolina in the Age of Jim Crow, required multiple "pedagogies" that were often spontaneous, contradictory, and varied, as well as being in response to or shaped by social oppression and inequalities. While some practices may certainly work today, I want to caution that these teachers worked under particular and unique conditions that could not simply be transplanted to the very different world of classrooms, schools, or communities today.

Remembering Pedagogical Responses

Generating Materials and Supplies: "You Had To Be Ingenious To Teach Then"

White educational authorities controlled the allocation of materials and supplies (tangible resources) that went to black schools, but they could not maintain control of the beliefs and practices (intangible resources) that teachers employed in their classrooms. When asked about the lack of resources that have now become entrenched in collective memories of Jim Crow schools, Effie Smith recounted: "Although we knew that we were getting second-hand materials, [black children] were not getting second-hand education. They were getting second-hand materials! When I say that we were teachers and that we went to teachers' colleges that meant that we knew about all the methods in teaching and the learning styles of the black kid." Born in Edgecombe County, Smith was reared and educated in the coastal plain region of North Carolina. After completing her degree in elementary education from Fayetteville State Teachers College (FSTC)—less than a two hour drive from her home—Smith began her teaching career using outdated books and inadequate supplies. In her interview, however, Smith recalled that FSTC teacher-training lab schools prepared its teachers for work in poor black rural schools. Additionally, growing up on "the colored side of the tracks," Smith had an insider's view of under-funded and legally segregated schools for blacks. All of the teachers I interviewed highlighted meager materials and supplies as one of the worst memories about teaching before integration, such as "hand-me-down" textbooks, used construction paper, poorly repaired buses, and dilapidated chalkboards. But these material things did not prevent them from facilitating the acquisition of educational capital among their students.

Participants explained how the lack of resources fostered creativity and resourcefulness which led to "situated" responses to very basic needs. In a reference to the first school where she taught in Nash County, Athalene Emory reported:

> the facility was not all that great. I had senior English and we were down in the basement of the gym. ... They talk about you have to have small class sizes, when I started out, I taught every senior at Nash County Training School in the basement and I guess there must have been 50-something students there. But I didn't know anything different. ... You come up with strategies that work and it was very workable.

Rather than over-emphasize what children and schools lacked, participants reported the ways in which they responded to institutional and structural barriers. Participants recalled very specific ways in which they had to be creative and resourceful:

The books that we were teaching out of were already five years behind the whites. I'm talking about before integration. So, you had to take that textbook and fit it to all those different groups. I more or less would rewrite the textbook for all my different groups.

(Fannie Coston)

The librarian would tell me when she was getting ready to discard dictionaries. I would send 10 or 12 boys out there to intercept them at the dumpsters and bring those dictionaries back to my room.

(Josephine Edwards)

Participants in my study do not disagree that some all-black schools were "inferior" to all-white schools, when you consider the systematic unequal funding of these schools and the neglect by white educational authorities. Annie Beasley stated candidly, "Well, I think that some of the education that all of us as black people received was inferior to what we received after integration, because we were not exposed to the materials that were available in the [white] schools or wherever. Some places you could not go to get the materials, even if you wanted it, because you were black." Both Mildred Hines and Mary Odom talked about teachers instructing in buses because of a shortage of classrooms and space in overcrowded black schools. Similarly, Thelma Forbes recalled her first teaching job in which she taught fifth graders in a long hallway because there were not enough classrooms. By the time most participants started teaching in the early 1950s, however, the funding of black schools had improved due to legal agitation by the National Association for the Advancement of Colored People (NAACP) at every governmental level (Patterson, 2001). However, the point that participants in my study made is that the creativity and ingenuity of black teachers made the difference in the acquisition of educational capital in spite of unequal treatment and inferior things handed down to them.

For example, Annie Beasley also recalled that she subscribed to *Readers Digest*, a widely circulated family magazine with stories, cartoons, brainteasers, and interviews. "*Readers Digest* had that good vocabulary section in there that I always used with my students. Anything that I thought could help them, I made copies of it and made it a part of my class."[4] Jessie Jones, who taught math and chemistry at the high school level, explained, "Inequality came from most basically not having equipment and supplies to work with but we used what was around; there was a lot of outdoor teaching that you could do with [trigonometry] you see. You didn't have all the basic equipment that you needed to teach [trigonometry] but you could go outside and teach for days. . . . we did science on a shoe string [budget]. They had to bring in the chemicals they had to work with—like baking soda, vinegar, and starch and all kinds of things like that because you couldn't afford all those chemicals." In another interview, Cleveland Lewis affirmed, "Black teachers in all-black schools were no way inferior. Black teachers worked and they demanded that the children got what they [needed]. The thing was that we just didn't have the equipment and stuff that they had at the white schools. But what we had, we used it." Clearly, participants did not feel totally defeated by the lack of materials and supplies.

The teachers themselves were the main resource through which educational capital was produced. All of the teachers I interviewed had been educated along the color line, attending all-black primary and grammar schools as well as colleges. They shared a common norm and expectation that permeated disadvantaged all-black schools: "We will climb though the rocks be rugged."[5] Catherine Taylor commented, "Working in the black schools, we didn't have everything that we needed; but, the black teachers, then, learned to do without and if you needed something you figured out how to get it. We spent our own money. Well, teachers still do that now. If we had had more money, maybe then, we would not have been as resourceful." One of the teachers who had been in charge of supplies and equipment in her school, Catherine Hines reflected: "We just didn't see that we were any worse off being a black school, because we had not been in their schools and really didn't know what they had to work with." Ada Pulley stated in her interview: "In spite of poor materials, you had to improvise. We are survivors! The black race [is full of] survivors. Just like I told you about my brother who has a Ph.D. in Linguistics, he went to a four room country school. You didn't have all these books. The elaborate building will not instruct, but the magic ingredient that creates a good learning situation, out of these meager supplies and things, is the relationships that exist and your determination." In this last account, notice that Pulley linked her brother's Ph.D. with the kind and quality of education that he received in what many would have called an "inferior" all-black school.

In Chapter 3, I discussed how black teachers financed and subsidized the all-black school across counties. There are numerous examples in the data about the amount of money that teachers spent for their classrooms and schools that simply cannot be overstated. Athalene Emory recalled: "The other thing about those days is that we had to be ingenious to teach then because we did not have the kinds of materials that you would have wanted. We had to buy most of these things and many of our children, they lived in poverty and the few pennies that we were making we had to spend on them." Hazel Lewis remembered: "We had to do fundraising. The teachers were responsible for doing some fundraising which after integration it became the PTO's responsibility to do fundraising. All schools had it. I mean nobody said you had to but every black teacher knew." Without participants generating materials and supplies out of their own pockets and through fundraisers, then a large number of students would not have been exposed to the knowledge and skills that prepared many of them to enroll in colleges and universities. Every participant who spoke specifically about spending money on materials and supplies also emphasized that resource deprivation did not stop teaching and learning. Despite the lack of tangible resources, these accounts suggest that teachers believed their teaching methods and practices to be sound and effective. They possessed hope over despair which guided their teaching and later has shaped the way that they recall their teacher experiences.

Beyond purchasing pencils, erasers, and workbooks, participants also talked about the physical, psychological, and emotional energy involved in generating supplies and material. For example, Amanda Cameron told a story about one of her male colleagues who refused to accept the textbooks that white administrators gave to their school:

> Mr. Fugett [white superintendent] told Mr. Johnson [black principal], 'look we got a lot of good books over here and we think your students could use them. There might be a few that you don't want to use. So he said you just send someone over and get these books.' And, who did he send, Coach Reid—Coach Reid told the story that he took every last one of them to the dump pile.

Coach Reid's account, as told by Amanda Cameron, suggests that black teachers were not as docile as some scholars have claimed. In fact, there was a "fire in the belly" of some teachers which demanded equal treatment or nothing. Some teachers bought and generated their own resources rather than spend a lot of time and energy fighting a "racist white school board," as many teachers referred to them. Similar to Sam Gray's story in the previous chapter about confronting the white school board about the use of the public park for athletic events, other teachers said that they would have fought more vigorously had it not been for black principals. For example, T.V. Foster mentioned a situation in which he asked for the most basic of materials for his classroom:

> I can recall I was teaching at Lincoln School and my classroom was under the stage and the blackboards that were in there had been brought over from another white school. The condition of [the blackboards] was so bad after a couple of years that I requested [replacements]. The principal at that time put in the request and the blackboards that the maintenance department brought over were also blackboards that had come out of a white school or had been used in a black school. The condition of those blackboards really was not good and I refused to accept them. They did give me new blackboards but I was reprimanded by the principal.

Dianne Turner, who later became a high school guidance counselor, remembered:

> I tell you another thing that I remember too, you know like when they had to administrate any type of achievement test, there were not enough

test booklets to go around and they would take the students and they would go to the gym. Teachers would take turns reading that test. You may have about a hundred kids in there and the teachers would take turns reading the test to them.

All of the solutions to resource problems were responses to a geopolitical climate in which teachers lived and worked. Even when black teachers were willing to fight or at least to go beyond the call of duty to generate materials and supplies for schools, some black principals demanded that they cease action or be fired. There is a need for more systematic research on the predicament of black principals in the Age of Jim Crow, in addition to early work on black principals conducted by Frederick Rodgers (1975) and recent work conducted by Randolph (2004) and Siddle Walker (2009). It is very likely that black principals simply did not want to deal with powerful white educational authorities. As Rodgers concluded: "The black principal was expected to avoid antagonizing the white community and its power structure while providing services that facilitated the progress and interests of the black community. If he violated the expectations of the former, he would be unceremoniously removed and 'blackballed' as an educator, and if he violated the expectations of the latter, he would be ostracized and despised by those whom he served" (p. 51).

Situating Curriculum and Instruction: "That Curriculum Was Not Designed For Poor Students"

Data revealed teaching practices that did not blame the students themselves or their home culture for "not learning" the curriculum. As Herbert Pulley recounted, "One thing that helped me more than anything that I have learned about methods of teaching is what an old college professor said, 'if the student hasn't learned, then the student hasn't been taught. So, that put the monkey on the teacher's back. . . . He would emphasize this in our teacher training. And, that was my mentality about teaching." Herbert's account, and others, shed light on an important question that I raised earlier: Considering the social, cultural, and economic predicament of poor and rural black children under Jim Crow, how might black teachers have understood educational barriers to black achievement and success?

Participants did not believe that students were doomed because they lacked cultural capital. They did believe, however, that without qualifications (in the form of skills, knowledge, and credentials) black students would have very few life chances due to skin color prejudice and social location in the Jim Crow South. In her interview, for example, Catherine Taylor explained:

> We didn't take the child and teach the child and when the child fails [pause] it is everybody's fault that the child fails—the child isn't dumb— the child isn't ignorant—the child is untaught.

Similarly, Helen Toney recalled:

> When children entered school, they had not been exposed to books, magazines, scissors, and they did not have pencils, pens, or anything. They had not been to kindergarten or day care. They had been at home with their mothers. You had to teach all the skills. How to hold a pencil. How to write. Learn your ABCs. Learn your phonics. Learn to count. So, they made a lot of progress but you had to consider from where they came.

Over time, small pedagogical acts in the classroom contributed to the acquisition of skills and knowledge for future success and opportunities.

Siddle Walker (1996a, 1996b) has written extensively about the extracurricular activities and programs in the all-black school which teachers linked to students' future opportunities. In the same way, Josephine Edwards remembered: "We were assigned chapel programs [in which] every Friday we would go to the auditorium for children to perform. I think that was a good thing because it enabled children to get up there before an audience and you would be surprised at the talent that the children had." While many of these activities were intended to build upon natural talent and leadership skills, other programs involved goal-setting and career exploration beyond "Negro jobs." Some participants reported:

> We brought in a lot of resources from the community to let the children know that these are some of the things that you can do—the dentist, the doctors, whatever profession these people were in. Students who had graduated from high school and had come back from college–and they were doing well—were given time to talk to the student body.
>
> (Athalene Emory)

> We would have a lot of speakers coming in and, you know, cats in the cradle. 'Momma, I am going to be like him because I like the way he talks. I like the way he is—nobody can put him down.' ... And, you were sort of proud to be a part of that group—most importantly, you just thought about the day you would go to college or you would further your education and be a little better off than what you were.
>
> (Nellie Hunter)

Alongside the job or career-related programming in these accounts, teachers encouraged the use of good English in Speech and Debate clubs, introduced their students to classical music in band and operettas, and encouraged athleticism in basketball and baseball teams. According to Rodgers (1975), "the extensiveness of the black high school's extracurricular activity program was more or less dependent on geographic location (city or rural) and size (large or small)" (p. 39).

Extracurricular activities and programs were definitely one area in which the lines between educational and cultural capital were blurred. Notably, elementary teachers in their seventies and eighties at the time of the interview recalled that classroom teachers carried out religious instruction. In an interview with T.V. Foster and Julia Foster, I discovered elaborate religious programming built into the school day:

Julia Foster: I told you about the daily devotions—the scripture and prayer.
Kelly: Briefly. Were there any teachers who refused?
T.V. Foster: No. There was no such thing. Integration brought along the end of [prayer].
Kelly: So, before integration, it was pretty much a part of school culture in the all-black schools to have devotions?
Julia Foster: Yes, that is right.
T.V. Foster: One thing about having devotion is the subtle impact that it had on the child. He kind of got in his mind that this is going to be a good day.

When I probed to find out more about devotion services as a part of the daily curriculum, Julia Foster explained: "well, we had devotion every morning. And that is when children were taught social behavior to a certain extent. And they realized they were taught to pray for help from our heavenly father and that really made a significant impression on their behavior.... Children were very respectful of the teachers because their teachers had control over them." Helen Toney recounted, "we had devotion every morning. I taught them music. I taught them songs every morning.... I taught them a morning prayer and a grace to say everyday before lunch." Although T.V. Foster stated that "integration brought along the end of that," there were no participants at the high school level and no participants in their fifties and sixties at the time of the interview who talked about devotion services. However, as Chapter 2 documented, most participants talked about attending church services in the larger communities which they also believed had a subtle impact on curriculum and instruction. As the hidden transcript reveals clearly, the home, school, and community were interconnected (See also Foster, 1991; Noblit and Dempsey, 1996; Siddle Walker, 1996).

Participants believed that the educational capital that all students acquired needed to be grounded in "racial knowledge" that would help them endure the world outside the black community. They prepared students with skills and knowledge combined with good moral development, a positive racial identity, and a solid basic education to enter a world of state-sponsored segregation, racial discrimination, and economic deprivation. For example, participants recalled:

> We didn't teach textbooks. Nor did we teach to tests. But we taught students as I hate to say it, but the whole child. It has become such a cliché. How do you teach half a child? But, we met students' needs—more so than they are doing now—not only educationally, but also socially, morally, spiritually. Whatever we saw that they needed to become a productive citizen, this is what we gave them.
>
> (E.J. Cummings)

> It wasn't just the Tigris and Euphrates rivers, you know. It also had to do with [racial pride]. 'Why [is] your hair is so pretty? Because God didn't make anything ugly. God gave you the hair that you have in order to fit the climate of Africa ... God gave you pretty hair and God made everything beautiful. So, don't let me see you sitting in the classroom and whining in reference to somebody's hair because it is straight. Yours wasn't meant to be straight. So, this was my way of teaching history: who you are and the beauty of you.
>
> (Nellie Hunter)

These accounts and others should make us wonder whether all the textbooks, materials, and supplies in the world could have replaced the role of Jim Crow's teachers, especially when you consider the form and content of the educational capital that teachers incorporated in the curriculum—racial pride, morality, responsibility, and citizenship.

Unfortunately, however, the general curricula appeared to have overlooked students with special needs across the three counties. Participants reported that special education was not a part of the all-black school until the late 1960s. Before special education programs, students with special needs, at the elementary level, were placed in "regular" classes at the elementary level and, at the junior high and high school levels, were typically placed in the bottom group. Anniebelle Ricks provided a general description of grouping at the junior and high school levels throughout Wilson County: "The A group was that top group who were going to college, the B group was average students who could go to college, and the C group was the slow learners." Some schools may not have used an alphabetical system, but the logic of the "C" group existed across counties. Herbert Pulley explained, "See back then, every child was encouraged to do your very best. And, that was my philosophy when I became a counselor, maybe you are not college material, go find out." Likewise, Dianne Turner remarked, "That curriculum was not designed *for* poor students because everybody was expected to do it. ... I didn't know what their economic background was, because it did not matter, I was expecting them to succeed. I didn't care where they came from [pause] and that was a glorious thing too." Had the curriculum been designed *for* poor students, especially poor and rural black students, teachers might have colluded unintentionally with white educational authorities who imagined black education for second class citizenship. The push and pull of preparing students with educational capital for respectability, I believe, worked against special needs students.

Some participants had clear recollections about the implementation of special education in the all-black school. Gloria Burks, a former music teacher who earned certification in special education (emotionally mentally handicapped and learning disabilities) founded the first program in her school district. In her own words, Burks talked about how she became involved in a movement to implement special education:

> I saw a need [pause] that the kids needed me in math, language, and reading worse than they did the music because they were going to get the music whether it was in church or on the radio. But you can't get that [math and reading] any other place other than someone teach you how to do math and reading. So, I went back to school. . . . Ben Toney and I started special education in this county—that was way back in '67 at Frederick Douglass. They gave us a room without books—nothing. We went into the library to get some discarded books and we picked up math books from here or there and got started that way.

When I asked how teachers dealt with special needs students before integration, Burks recalled: "Out of 4 or 5 classes, I will say you might have 3 people who we knew were kind of slow—but we wouldn't say it." While my research looked at curriculum and instruction generally, there is a need for more systematic research to get a fuller picture of how black teachers before integration dealt with special needs students beyond the anecdotal evidence that I have provided here. When you consider the active role of the politics of respectability in black life and culture, black teachers' work might have been shaped by a social climate in which blacks were unable or unwilling to acknowledge weaknesses or vulnerabilities within the race.

Remembering Pedagogic Initiatives

Mobilizing Resources: "We Meant Business."

Before integration, teachers and principals formed a system of checks and balances that created stable environments across generations. Each of them became a mobilizing resource to make up for the lack of tangible resources that existed in legally segregated schools for blacks. While the coordination and connectedness of "human resources" was important, interviews revealed that teachers and principals also needed to be committed—time, energy, money, hope—to students and families. In other words, the success of their efforts depended upon the support of multiple groups (e.g., parents, churches, and civic organizations) working with teachers. I have provided accounts of parents as a major resource in the previous chapter, which is a common theme throughout existing studies (Siddle Walker, 2000). This particular section continues to explore the hidden contributions of "teachers" but also the combined effort of black principals. The more people engaged, I argue, the more tangible and intangible resources were made available in the all-black school.

The black teachers I interviewed were clearly a major resource to the intellectual development of black students in Jim Crow schools. Oral narratives revealed hidden contributions by individual teachers that often went unnoticed and unrewarded by white educational authorities. Most students who attended all-black schools before integration were probably not aware of the expert knowledge and credentials that teachers and principals brought to teaching and learning. Throughout the Jim Crow years, according to participants, the state of North Carolina required black and white teachers to earn college credits for professional development (Siddle Walker, 1996b). Those teachers who did not earn graduate degrees paid "out of their pockets" for continuing education courses. Amanda Cameron, for instance, reported that she took a summer course on the "the slow learner" before there was even a special education program in her county. These individual acts to acquire more educational capital brought many teachers into collective action across counties.

Some participants, like Amanda Cameron, did not obtain advanced degrees but they spent summers completing coursework in the latest methods in teaching. Of the forty-four teachers that I interviewed, twelve received a master's degree before school integration. Seven received their master's degrees after integration, with one participant earning a doctorate in curriculum and instruction from Duke University. Appendix C provides more details about the graduate institutions that participants attended. Such flows of ideas and information facilitated the acquisition of educational capital among their students in spite of "savage inequalities" at the local level. As teachers acquired more educational capital themselves, which Chapter 3 indicated, they could have left the K-12 classroom for careers at the college-level or sought employment in governmental jobs through civil service tests.[6] However, my participants continued to work in all-black schools and communities. Even participants who never married and earned advanced degrees made a decision to stay in teaching because of their attachments and commitment to the children and families that they served.

Across schools and counties, participants uncovered educational philosophies which they believed shaped their thinking about students, families, and teaching during the Jim Crow years:

> It was a calling, not so much a profession. Anybody can get a profession but somebody has to have a calling and somebody has to go in and

love the people. You realize that somebody needs you to help them and I had the calling.

(Nellie Hunter)

It was very much the same kind of atmosphere there that I had at Booker T—the faculty was extremely close—we did everything together—everybody was pro student. What can we do that will make these students [successful] so that they don't have to stay in the circumstances that they are in now?

(Athalene Emory)

We did not just do what we were being paid for. We went above and beyond to see that children were treated right and got a good education.

(Ada Pulley)

While I have argued that teachers were an important resource within schools, teachers' efforts depended upon the cooperation of black principals, parents and community members.

What Irvine (1989) has described as "cultural synchronization," I argue, also came out of a political commitment to dispel the myth of black inferiority. Teachers, parents, and principals worked together to mobilize resources and to provide home and school structures that supported teachers and teaching. Dianne Turner remarked, "when we walked in that schoolhouse you could look at us and tell—students and teachers—we meant business. Teachers were dressed professionally. Some of the kids even came to school with shirts and ties on." Accordingly, there was an emphasis on excellence and the importance of being respectable. Across all three counties, parents, teachers, and the principal created and maintained school cultures in which dress and deportment went hand in hand with the acquisition of educational capital in their effort to educate the "whole child."

Overwhelmingly, the 44 participants in this study stated that there were few behavior problems in the all-black school before integration. For example, participants remembered:

> We had little discipline problems. All you had to do was contact the parents. [imitating] 'You know what, I am going to send your parent a little note.' And, they knew that they better give it to the parent. That is all you had to do.
>
> (Amanda Cameron)

> Somehow or other you would tell them, 'you better bring that assignment, you better have it tomorrow.' And if she was really upset, then the teacher would go to your house because everybody didn't have telephones. She would go to the house and it was oh Lord, here come the teacher. Oh Lord, is right. If somebody would see her in the

neighborhood—I saw Miss Jones. Lord, have mercy, I hope she doesn't go to my house.

(Gloria Burks)

Well as far as discipline was concerned you rarely had any problem with discipline because many times the word got home before you did. . . . They took the D out of the schools—discipline.

(Henry Davis)

The teacher could do no wrong and the students knew it—as a result you didn't have any—not that many kids, you know, caused a problem and they were pretty successful and the parents were with you at the PTAs and coming out to school.

(Vera Tyson)

One could argue that those children were different from children today. However, teachers that I interviewed talked about a changing structure in the school and changing relationships between home and school as the key factors explaining today's discipline problems.

Participants acknowledged that black principals made sure that the all-black school was a place of teaching and learning. According to Athalene Emory, "When we were in the all-black situation, we had principals who were extremely well-educated. They were men who were not only educated academically but they were extremely well-educated in so far as social things that students needed." When I probed for more clarity about what she meant by "social things" she compared her experiences with two principals she worked with before integration:

Athalene: The two principals had the same kind of style and as I said before I think all of the principals—the black principals at that time were men who had been not only academically trained but were well-rounded.
Interviewer: Charismatic?
Athalene: Yes. Right. They were very charismatic men. But they were gentlemanly—I guess that is the word that I want to use—all of them—carried the same kind of air and their dispositions were the same. There was not two cents worth of difference between O.R. Pope and Ed Barnes.

Similarly, Alton Bobbitt described his principal in a "gentlemanly" way but also as the kind of person who could go out into the tobacco fields with "overalls" on and seek support from local farmers.

While teachers said that they respected their principals, most did not like them very much. Cleveland Lewis recalled, "back during that time you see when you got a job you had to keep your mouth shut. They had a hammer over your head and the least little thing that was said, you would be gone. You would be fired in a split second. And that was it." Josephine Edwards remarked, "black teachers caught holy hell." Dianne Turner stated, "just like there were rules for students, there were rules for teachers." In sum, everyone had a role to play, and resources to give, in the daily drama of educating black youth in the coastal plain of Jim Crow North Carolina.

FORGING DOUBLE CONSCIOUSNESS: "YOU ARE TRYING TO BUILD YOUR PEOPLE UP."

Ultimately, participants believed that they were forging a new way of being in the world for the black race. In interviews, I asked each participant to tell me what they expected to read in a book about black teachers before integration. E. J. Cummings' response captures the overall sentiments of participants in the study:

> I would certainly expect to read in that book and now here I can't speak globally because I don't know what the teaching was like in Mississippi—I don't know what the teaching was like in Louisiana—I really don't know. But the teachers in North Carolina were prepared to do the job. And, they did their job. . . . They understood the black child and they worked with the black child to cultivate a child that was capable of holding his own not only educational wise but culturally in the community and they taught children to become good, productive worthwhile citizens who felt that no man was their superior because he was white and no man was inferior because he was black.

Like this former teacher and principal, participants talked about themselves as part of a collective social project which sought to change the way the black race was perceived and experienced.

At the local level, I argue, white supremacy created a cultural dilemma and pedagogical tension for teachers in the Age of Jim Crow: educate black youth to be a Negro or to be an American. Historically, Leon Litwack (1979) has pointed out, across the political spectrum, just being a "Negro" meant that you possessed "low status" and merited second-class citizenship in the minds of white southerners. As a racial signifier, regardless of class or gender, black skin color alone could trigger racial hostility, discrimination, and often violence in white public space. After the Civil War, for example, newly freed slaves were ridiculed and threatened with violence for imitating whites when they walked around town dressed in their best clothes or struggled to send their children to school rather than the field (Litwack, 1979). In North Carolina, and throughout the Jim Crow South, blacks who flaunted dominant high status culture could easily be branded an uppity nigger, taunted, tortured, and/or killed (Litwack, 1998; Packard,

2002). Recognizing the real consequences of being perceived as "uppity" by whites, black teachers were cautious and responsible in their efforts to promote respectability and cultivate a double consciousness among their students.

In *The Souls of Black Folk*, Du Bois was the first to articulate the very essence of this cultural dilemma as "double consciousness." Du Bois (1903/1994, p. 5) wrote:

> It is a peculiar sensation, this double-consciousness, this sense of always looking at one's self through the eyes of others, of measuring one's soul by the tape of a world that looks on in amused contempt and pity. One ever feels his two-ness—An American, a Negro; two souls, two thoughts, two unreconciled strivings; two warring ideals in one dark body, whose dogged strength alone keeps it from being torn asunder.

Although participants did not use the term "double consciousness" to convey their double aims of racial pride and racial etiquette, the concept emerged from the data in their explanations of how they prepared students for both a black and white world. Historian David Levering Lewis (1993) explained that "in *Souls* the divided self would not remain flawed, compromised, unstable, or tragic. It would become in time and struggle stronger for being doubled, not undermined—the sum of its parts, not the dividend" (p. 282). It is from this perspective that I employ DuBois's concept of double consciousness, or racial twoness, to examine how black teachers before integration approached the task of providing educational capital—cautiously and responsibly.

In the South, black teachers could not produce "uppity" Negroes, nor could they train "second-class citizens." Participants' accounts revealed that black teachers supported a healthy double consciousness in which students struggled against white cultural practices but also sought to defy white supremacist ideology. Participants gave school-wide and classroom examples of how a healthy double consciousness got promoted, for example:

> The students would march into the auditorium on baccalaureate or graduation night and you would see this big old sign, "Not finished just beginning." And often they would say "a little bit of learning is a dangerous thing." But you know a few words can make you think. I am not finished here tonight—I am just beginning—I am going on to college—I am going to some school you know and further my education.
> (Nellie Hunter)

> But then what you are trying to do, you are trying to build your people up. You see what is going on, trying to prepare them for tomorrow so

they can go out there and do better than you. Now our job was trying to prepare them for tomorrow you see.

(Henry Davis)

We were always taught that we were just as good as anybody. And, my parents instilled in us that the way you carry yourself is what counts. We never looked down or held our heads down. We always held our heads up.

(Ada Pulley)

As DuBois foresaw, participants were creating a "respectable" race through the quickening and training of human intelligence, or what I call the acquisition of educational capital. Whether it was the use of a school motto, a common goal to prepare students for tomorrow rather than today, or a directive to hold your head up, teachers sought to instill ambition, hope, and pride in their students. In this way, the skills, knowledge, and credentials that students possessed would not only work in the interest of individuals but also in the interest of the race.

Double consciousness provided a counter-discourse, which enabled some black teachers to challenge white supremacy and white racism directly in the school. Although the account that I am about to describe did not change the power structure at all, there is some evidence of a racial consciousness and a demand for respect among the teachers I interviewed. In addition, this account can give us a sense of the likely racial uplift work that teachers practiced in their classrooms. For example, Anniebelle Ricks told a story about how Amanda Mitchell Cameron—whom I later interviewed—scolded the white school superintendent in a faculty meeting. Apparently, on one of his rare visits to their school, the white superintendent gave a speech in which he kept referring to the entire black faculty as "niggras." Cameron was so disturbed by the superintendent's tone and his "intentional" mispronunciation of "Negro" that she raised her hand in the middle of his speech to the faculty. The superintendent stopped to take her question. Amanda said, "Mr. Humphreys. Can you say "HERO?" According to Ricks, everyone's eye's dropped to their knees. After a quick, "yes," from the superintendent, Cameron continued, "well, Mr. Humphreys, you should be able to say "NEGRO." Ricks remembered that the entire faculty was on pins and needles; they were amused by Cameron's reprimand of the superintendent but they also feared she would be fired. In her interview, Ricks speculated that Cameron was not fired because her father was a "big time" farmer, who owned a lot of land in the community. When I asked her about the risk involved, Cameron remarked:

> "Wonder that I had not been fired. You know, at the time, we didn't know anything about what the Board [of Education] [was] doing because it was a lily white Board. All we had to do when the superintendent

was coming over [pause] you know you got almost like tense—the superintendent is coming! . . . You had to be careful. I guess sometimes I would, at least, I would forget that. And then, I think they were afraid to fire me because my daddy was a tax payer in this county. . . . if you didn't own anything, you were just about a nothing, you know. So, I guess I might have said a lot of things and got away with them more than maybe someone else because my daddy was a landowner.

Cameron's use of language to make a point is important here. Instead of confronting power directly, she chose to correct the way the white superintendent pronounced the word "Negro." After all, the situation was a power laden one. Was it not the duty of competent teachers to encourage the use of good speech, grammar, and pronunciation? Of course, Cameron actually sought to correct the disrespectful way that the white superintendent treated her and her colleagues. But it is important to note that Cameron drew upon her own double consciousness to disrupt a racist act. Still, she recognized the limits of her resistance to white power. While it was not completely safe, it was hardly reproachable when you consider that the superintendent was addressing a group of college-educated faculty.

Black teachers in my study pushed educational capital as the accepted mode of social mobility because they saw skills, knowledge, and credentials as a weapon against white supremacy. Still, the question remains: did cultural capital alone explain black students' success or failure? The short answer can be read from participant's actual transcripts in which many stated an idiom that they had been told by their parents and teachers: "education is something the white man can't take away from you." They understood that education would further expose their students to the world beyond Jim Crow North Carolina. Participants suggested that what black youth needed, second to "material and supplies," before integration was "exposure." The type of exposure they described was not imitative of white culture, nor was it necessarily the acquisition of white high brow culture. Rather, it included an awareness of the black and white world but maintained self-respect, self-knowledge, and self-reliance in opposition to white supremacy. By these standards, the successful black person acquired educational capital with strong black cultural affirmation and a double consciousness for survival in a segregated world.

Throughout much of his writing at the turn of the century, and beyond, it is quite clear that DuBois encouraged educational capital as long as it was grounded in black cultural affirmation and double consciousness. For example, DuBois (1903/2002) wrote: "As long as the Negro student wishes to graduate from Columbia, not because Columbia is an institution of learning, but because it is attended by white students; as long as a Negro student is ashamed to attend Fisk or Howard because these institutions are largely run by black folk, just so long, the main problem of Negro education will not be segregation but self-knowledge and self-respect" (p. 138). Instead of combining educational capital with a focus on acquiring white high status signals, the black teachers in my study practiced situated pedagogies whereby students were expected to forge a healthy double consciousness.

By generating materials and supplies, situating curriculum and instruction, mobilizing resources and nurturing a double consciousness with students, participants promoted the acquisition of educational capital for jobs, civil rights, and social power. Ultimately, I contend that they possessed a critique of power rooted in the social, cultural, and geopolitical realities of the Jim Crow South that led to strategies of opportunity. Despite the negatives that they faced—educational barriers, resource deprivation, and white supremacy—black teachers in my study believed that they were quite successful when you consider the sum total of skills, knowledge, and credentials bestowed upon multiple generations of black youth.

Part III
Remembering Jim Crow's Teachers

6 "The Half Had Not Been Told"
Hidden Transcripts Made Public

Drawing upon the collective remembering of former teachers of legally segregated schools for blacks, I have examined both "how" and "what" they remember about teachers and teaching in the coastal plain of North Carolina. First and foremost, participants in my study—individually and collectively—drew upon hidden transcripts to recall "remarkably good" memories of the all-black school before integration. Second, given that hidden transcripts mediate how former teachers remember, participants revealed pedagogical responses and initiatives to the geopolitics of race and racism that critiqued white racism and advanced the acquisition of educational capital. In addition to well-documented educational barriers, participants remembered undocumented, unknown, and unacknowledged ways in which they prepared poor and working-class black youth for a dual labor market and for a world beyond a segregated black society.

As part of the legacy of Jim Crow's teachers, participants in my study used schools as spaces of constant possibility and contestation. Considering the social, geopolitical, and economic predicament in which teachers worked in the coastal plain of North Carolina, the public transcript of "inherently inferior" all-black schools does not tell the whole story of teaching and learning within segregated classrooms and schools. As Scott (1990) duly noted, "every subordinate group creates, out of its ordeal, a hidden transcript that represents a critique of power spoken behind the back of the dominant" (xii). The primary purpose of this book has been to establish the quality and character of teachers and teaching in legally segregated schools for blacks by listening to the voices of collective remembering among former teachers and uncovering hidden transcripts that they make public decades after the power structure has changed and powerful people are no longer living. Moreover, I document "offstage gestures and practices that confirm, contradict, or inflect what appears in the public transcript" (Scott, 1990, p. 4). In this chapter, I conclude the book with a brief evaluation of participants' beliefs and actions as read and interpreted from their oral narratives. I also discuss two foundational principles that are useful and necessary to live by as we continue to educate disadvantaged youth with paltry resources and unequal funding in resegregated schools.

GEOPOLITICAL REALITIES AND LIMITATIONS

During and following the integration of public schools in all three counties, participants in my study engaged in formal and informal discussions about the way things used to be in their all-black schools. Some of these conversations were rehearsed in living rooms and around kitchen tables with former co-workers, in the hallways and classrooms in a newly integrated school, or at civic and church gatherings with the next generation of teachers, administrators, and students (See also, Liberato, Fennell, & Jeffries, 2008). Since the narratives that participants recalled had been told and retold among themselves since the official close of the all-black public school, the oral interviews that I conducted are hidden transcripts that I have made public through this book. In the retelling of their hidden stories and strategies, however, what has been lost is the social and geopolitical context in which these teachers worked. A simple retelling of historical dates and events cannot capture what was at stake in the Age of Jim Crow. Thus, I continue the "autobiographical sketch" that I started in Chapter 2 from Richard Wright's "The Ethics of Living Jim Crow." Wright's written narrative illuminates the geopolitical situation as teachers explained it to me which can be lost in a "reading" of their hidden transcripts. Wright's story recapitulates the promise and the perils of teachers' work as a geopolitical practice in the coastal plain of North Carolina, which ultimately depended upon the benevolent deeds or malevolent actions of white authorities.

If you recall in Chapter 2, Wright began his story with the central character describing the very day that he learned what it meant to be a Negro in rural Arkansas. He had been imparted "Jim Crow wisdom" from his mother after a hard lesson in social interactions with white peers: "*She grabbed a barrel stave, dragged me home, stripped me naked, and beat me till I had a fever of one hundred and two. She would smack my rump with the stave, and, while the skin was still smarting, impart to me gems of Jim Crow wisdom. I was never to throw cinders any more. I was never to fight any more wars. I was never, never, under any conditions, to fight white folks again*" (Wright, 1937/ 2001, p.23). Choosing to end the sketch at the point of hope, I continue the story now to find out what happened after the central character's family had moved to Mississippi and became a part of an all-black community. Remember also that the central character had just been hired in a white-owned and operated optical company in Jackson Mississippi, due to his two years of Algebra and applying Jim Crow wisdom learned from his mother and others in his community.

Wright's (1937/2001) narrative continued:

> *I worked hard, trying to please. For the first month I got along O.K. Both Pease and Morrie seemed to like me. But one thing was missing. And I kept thinking about it. I was not learning anything, and nobody was volunteering to help me. Thinking they had forgotten that I was to*

> learn something about the mechanics of grinding lenses, I asked Morrie one day to tell me about the work. He grew red.
> 'Whut yuh tryin' t' do, nigger, git smart?' he asked.
> 'Naw; I ain' tryin' t' -it smart,' I said.
> 'Well, don't, if yuh know whut's good for yuh!'
> I was puzzled. Maybe he just doesn't want to help me, I thought. I went to Pease.
> 'Say, are you crazy, you black bastard?' Pease asked me, his gray eyes growing hard.
> I spoke out, reminding him that the boss had said I was to be given a chance to learn something.
> 'Nigger, you think you're white, don't you?'
> 'Naw, sir!'
> 'Well, you're acting mighty like it!'
> 'But, Mr. Pease, the boss said . . . '
> Pease shook his fist in my face.
> 'This is a white man's work around here, and you better watch yourself!'
> From then on they changed toward me. They said good-morning no more. When I was just a bit slow in performing some duty, I was called a lazy black son-of-a-bitch. (Wright, 1937/2001, p. 24)

Although the central character had "qualified" for a job in the optical company, he continued to be discriminated against by white co-workers who refused to train him, who were upset by his presence in the workplace, and who were also eager to put him in his place as a "nigger." Despite skills, knowledge, or credentials that the central character possessed, he was still considered a "lazy black son-of-a bitch." As the story continued, Wright ended this episode (there are ten in total) with a dispute that leads to the central character leaving his first job:

> Richard, Mr. Morrie here tells me you called me Pease.'
> I stiffened. A void seemed to open up in me. I knew this was the showdown.
> He meant that I had failed to call him Mr. Pease. I looked at Morrie. He was gripping a steel bar in his hands. I opened my mouth to speak, to protest, to assure Pease that I had never called him simply Pease, and that I had never had any intentions of doing so, when Morrie grabbed me by the collar, ramming my head against the wall.
> 'Now, be careful, nigger!' snarled Morrie, baring his teeth. 'I heard yuh call 'im Pease! 'N' if yuh say yuh didn't, yuh're callin' me a lie, see?' He waved the steel bar threateningly.
> If I had said: No, sir, Mr. Pease, I never called you Pease, I would have been automatically calling Morrie a liar. And if I had said: Yes, sir, Mr. Pease, I called you Pease, I would have been pleading guilty to having

> uttered the worst insult that a Negro can utter to a southern white man. I stood hesitating, trying to frame a neutral reply.
> 'Richard, I asked you a question!' said Pease. Anger was creeping into his voice.
> 'I don't remember calling you Pease, Mr. Pease,' I said cautiously. 'And if I did, I sure didn't mean . . .'
> 'You black son-of-a-bitch! You called me Pease, then!' he spat, slapping me till I bent sideways over a bench. Morrie was on top of me, demanding:
> 'Didn't yuh call 'im Pease? If yuh say yuh didn't, I'll rip yo' gut string loose with this f—kin' bar, yuh black granny dodger! Yuh can't call a white man a lie 'n' git erway with it, you black son-of-a-bitch!'
> I wilted. I begged them not to bother me. I knew what they wanted. They wanted me to leave.
> 'I'll leave,' I promised. 'I'll leave right now.'
> They gave me a minute to get out of the factory. I was warned not to show up again, or tell the boss.
> I went.
> When I told the folks at home what had happened, they called me a fool. They told me that I must never again attempt to exceed my boundaries. When you are working for white folks, they said, you got to "stay in your place" if you want to keep working. (Wright, 1937/2001, p. 24)

As in Chapter 2, the central character learned two principles in support of white hegemonic domination: "never again attempt to exceed [your] boundaries" and "stay in your place."

Ultimately, Wright's narrative directs our attention to the limits of educational capital as a strategy of opportunity. The central character had used his acquired skills and knowledge to secure a skilled job across the color line; however, racial prejudice and violence ruined his chances to succeed and compelled him to leave. Unlike the "folks at home" who passed along Jim Crow wisdom about how to survive the other side of the tracks (although they may have had a critique of power themselves), former teachers I studied were involved in daily acts of resistance in segregated all-black schools away from white educational authorities. Being "segregated," I argue, was important because it provided a social and intellectual space where resistance and counter-hegemonic ideals could flourish. More importantly, a collective will against white hegemonic domination could be formed.

In the Age of Jim Crow, the school became a site for counter-hegemonic acts and beliefs. My evaluation of the teachers I interviewed, as well as what I have taken from other counter-narratives, is that their pedagogical actions and beliefs were indeed counter-hegemonic. Outside the schoolhouse gates, however, teachers' efforts were limited by the realities of living Jim Crow which dictated the life chances of black youth despite the educational capital they had to exchange in the white dominant labor market. It would take the black civil rights movement to "change" the power structure so that skills, knowledge, and credentials could not only get black youth through the proverbial door, but also protect them on the other side of it.

Jim Crow's Teachers and Their Counter-Hegemonic Struggle

Under state-sponsored racial discrimination, teachers in my study promoted the acquisition of educational capital as the accepted mode of social mobility. They believed that what black youth needed was hard currency (skills, knowledge, and credentials through formal schooling) that could be used in a dual labor market. Although I have argued that they did not simply promote a "culture of respectability," participants did embrace a "politics of respectability" for skilled jobs, civil rights, and social power. The degree to which participants were successful cannot be determined easily, but I do believe that there is much to learn from (and about) their collective remembering. What I find most important is the image of these teachers as counter-hegemonic agents against public transcripts of them as apolitical and self-serving (for similar critiques, Fairclough, 2001, 2007; Siddle Walker, 2001, 2005).

Quality and Character of Teachers and Teaching

Across Edgecombe, Wilson, and Nash counties, teachers worked against a white supremacist hegemonic discourse of black inferiority and second-class citizenship. Instead of maintaining the status quo, teachers recalled a collective vision to create a different way of being in the world for the black race. Consequently, they remember teaching in the all-black school to be "exciting times" in which they were engaged in hard work—teaching and motivating black rural youth to complete high school and to seek a college education. Teachers saw their work as a geopolitical act with the goal of changing the racial landscape for their students through the acquisition of educational capital for exchange across the color line. Since these teachers were products of black schools and communities themselves, they became living testimonies that poor and working-class blacks could move off the farm into skilled and professional work.

Preparation of Black Youth for Skilled Jobs, Civil Rights, and Social Power

Teachers fashioned situated pedagogies that were mainly in response to or shaped by social oppression and inequalities. Intentionally, this book did not draw upon one type of situated pedagogy, such as culturally relevant pedagogy (Ladson-Billings, 1995) or politically relevant pedagogy (Beauboeuf-Lafontant, 1999). In addition, I have made no deliberate attempt to identify best teaching practices that can be bottled and sold for usage by classroom teachers today. The point I wish to make is that teachers created and responded to the socio-historical situation and circumstances of their time—the Age of Segregation. While some pedagogical practices may certainly work today, I want to caution that these teachers worked under particular and unique conditions that cannot be transplanted to the very different world of today's classrooms, schools, or communities.

At the close of the all-black public school, teachers in my study recalled collective responses and initiatives to state-sponsored educational barriers and racism such as generating materials and supplies, situating curriculum and instruction, mobilizing resources and forging a double consciousness. Each of these themes locates the problem of academic achievement and social mobility in structural constraints and educational barriers, not the lack of cultural capital due to an impoverished home culture. While many participants' efforts were hidden, more likely than not, they made a huge difference when you consider what the alternatives might have been.

Collective Remembering from Hidden Transcripts

Teachers possessed a collective memory of "good but not perfect" all-black public schools before integration. In oral interviews, participants recounted some hidden transcripts that no one wanted to be written into the book. For example, there were many female teachers who lost their jobs because they refused to "sleep" with the principal. Both male and female teachers were reluctant to talk about alleged sexual misconduct and harassment by male principals and some male teachers. Since I promised that these hidden transcripts would remain hidden—meaning that I would not give names or schools—I have mentioned this unexplored aspect of my own counter-narrative to acknowledge that not all hidden transcripts can be made public. While some teachers did think that now it would be fine to talk about "sexual misconduct" in the book, other teachers were adamant that "we don't need to let white folk know all of our business." The hidden transcripts that participants did want to make public, though, uncover a collective will and vision against hegemonic white domination.

Beyond collective remembering from experience, teachers drew upon hidden transcripts that were formed under particular social and geopolitical circumstances. Just as soldiers who recount war stories passed down from generation to generation, teachers in my study also told "school stories" from hidden transcripts across multiple generations. Participants were more than willing to make hidden transcripts about white supremacy and racism public, but they were less than willing to have narratives of sexism or hegemonic masculinity publicized. After all, some of these men and their family members are still living and contributing to the community.

"Back Down Memory Lane": Foundational Principles for the 21st Century in an Age of Resegregation

Oral interviews have uncovered numerous good and happy memories of the all-black school before integration as a valued social and intellectual space by students, teachers, parents, and community members alike. These "good" memories, however, should not be separated from the trials and tribulations that many former teachers in my study experienced in the form of state-sponsored racial discrimination, unequal funding between white and black schools, and closed opportunity structures in the labor market. Although there are public transcripts to support a profoundly negative collective memory of legally segregated schools for blacks, there are also public and hidden transcripts in the form of oral narratives and archival material to support extant counter-memories.

As the old saying goes, "the half had not been told." Clearly, it is not enough to accept what former teachers say at face value. I hope that I have provided enough convincing evidence to support my argument that black teachers before integration were a major resource for black achievement and social mobility. One of the limitations of the study is that I have no data to discuss outcomes, especially how successful teachers were beyond self-reports (e.g., high school and college graduate rates over time and changes in work/occupation type within the black population). What I do offer are some clues about the quality and character of teachers under power-laden circumstances (Chapter 3) and some strategies that teachers might employ to address societal and institutional problems in education (Chapter 4).

Although former teachers in legally segregated black public schools did not work under the same conditions that today's teachers face, growing research on the "re-segregation of public schools" in rural, suburban, and urban schools throughout the United States calls attention to important principles that should be understood from my study. According to a team of researchers at the Harvard University Civil Rights Project, now located at the University of California at Los Angeles, (Frankenberg and Lee, 2002; Frankenberg, Lee, & Orfield, 2003; Holley, 2005; Orfield, 2001; Orfield and Lee, 2005; Orfield and Monfort, 1988), there is a pervasive pattern of resegregation in U.S. public schools due mostly to the reversal of desegregation court orders and the increasing segregation of white, black and Latino neighborhoods and communities. Writing about segregated schools today, Frankenberg, Lee, & Orfield (2003) reported:

> Segregated schools have much higher concentrations of poverty and other problems and much lower average test scores, levels of student, teacher qualifications, and advanced courses. With few exceptions, separate schools are still unequal schools. Ending desegregation plans tends to produce a rapid increase of such schools within a district, and more qualified teachers tend to leave these segregated schools. (p. 11).

While the resegregation of public schools is beyond the scope of my research, I argue that it might be necessary to go "back down memory lane" to address some of the problems facing us today. Jim Crow's teachers, however, lived in a very different geopolitical and social world.

Good Neighbors

Today's teachers and administrators must become "good neighbors" to students and families in their school communities. The idea of good neighbors recognizes that there are problems with contemporary uses of the family metaphor in our increasingly diverse and complex society. Educational administrators and classroom teachers, for example, often describe their relationships with students and parents as "like a family" without knowing where students live or without ever meeting students' parents or guardians. As good neighbors, however, teachers can be welcoming to students who enter their classrooms from homes that are different from their own. Teachers can learn about the social background and home culture that students possess in order to adapt their curriculum and instruction to students' needs. Teachers can offer to help students and families navigate the school system, especially when they know that educational practices and policies have negative consequences for students, families and communities.

In classrooms and schools today, it is too easy for teachers to assume that "those" students and their personal troubles are not connected to my life. It is also too easy to blame "those" students or "their" parents for "their" socio-economic situation or location. Within rural, suburban and urban schools, teachers are working as strangers in the communities where they teach (despite racial or cultural matching) which has serious consequences for educating "other people's children" (Delpit, 1995). The end result may be that teachers, as strangers, maintain low expectations and fail to promote the acquisition of educational capital. In my study, however, teachers were of/from/in the communities in which they taught. While this particular point has been associated with notions of racial or cultural matching, I want to highlight that teachers *understood* the societal and structural problems that their students faced. Teachers fought against a common enemy to the life chances of black students in Jim Crow North Carolina.

Double Consciousness

Like good neighbors, teachers must relate to the lives of students and families next door because they are connected to them—geographically and politically. Teachers must also possess a double consciousness rooted in the geopolitical situation in which their students live. As Jonathan Kozol (2005) articulated well:

Teachers in these schools must work, and know that they must work, within "the box" of segregated demographics and extreme inequities . . . but in their temperaments and in their moral disposition many also stand outside that box, because they are aware of its existence, and this sense of double-vision, being part of something and aware of what it is at the same time, regenerates the energy they bring with them each morning to the very little place (one room, one set of chairs) in which they use what gifts they have to make the schoolday good and whole and sometimes beautiful for children." (p. 287).

In the contemporary United States, as Kozol inferred, teachers must craft their own situated pedagogies in which students are affirmed and they are encouraged to acquire educational capital **because of** complex inequalities shaping their lives. In addition, teachers must possess a collective will and vision for all students. The only other alternative for teachers, I argue, is having "no consciousness" which leads to cultural deficit thinking and strategies of despair. While I do recognize that some teachers possess a double consciousness but are overwhelmed by the lack of resources in their communities and schools, I encourage them to draw upon the hidden transcripts of Jim Crow's teachers for strategies of opportunity and narratives of hope in the unseen.

The time may never come when every child and every school is adequately funded, valued and supported. While there is a need for more people organizing to demand that every child has a right to quality education through the free public system, there is still a need for more teachers to develop situated pedagogies that lead to the acquisition of skills, knowledge and credentials for jobs, civil rights and social power (See also, Ladson-Billings, 2000; Lather and Ellsworth, 1996). The 44 teachers that I interviewed in the coastal plain of North Carolina provide an example of what teachers can do in schools that lack resources and support from local educational authorities. In the contemporary United States, teachers' must craft their own strategies of opportunity in which students' cultures are affirmed and whereby students leave classrooms with educational capital in spite of the complex inequalities that they are born into. As participants in my study have illustrated through their stories about teaching before school desegregation, they worked under some of the most difficult circumstances. Yet, they forged.

Appendix A

METHODOLOGY

This research draws upon oral history interviews, archival research, and secondary historical materials. I selected this state and geographic region for two reasons: one, several influential single-case and community studies (Cecelski, 1994; Noblit and Dempsey, 1996; Siddle Walker, 1996b; Philipsen, 1999) already exist about legally segregated schooling in North Carolina, which permits constant comparison and theory construction; and two, this is the place where I was born and raised so I am very familiar with the social and geopolitical terrain. Not only did I grow up in this area, but also I taught in a middle school in one of the counties in the late 1990s. Therefore, I had networks or connections that I could tap into to assist me in soliciting participants.

I conducted semi-structured interviews with 44 former classroom teachers who taught in all-black schools in three counties (Edgecombe, Nash, and Wilson) in the coastal plain region of North Carolina. I interviewed 14 males and 30 females, with an age range from 59 to 85. (See Appendix C for a table on demographic data and characteristics of the participants in the study.) All participants were asked open-ended questions, such as "What do you remember about teaching in all-black schools before integration?," "In the schools, where you taught, what do you remember about the quality of education children received?," and "What are your best and worst memories of teaching in all-black schools before integration?" In a conversational manner, participants answered questions about how they remembered their work before school integration.[1] Most of the interviews were conducted in the homes of participants, but three occurred in family-owned businesses. The interviews lasted approximately 90 minutes. None of the information about participants has been changed or altered. Nearly all of the teachers later taught in integrated schools; the only two exceptions are teachers who started second careers in black-owned businesses within black communities (i.e., a funeral home and a gas station/convenience store).

Appendix A

Oral History Interview Data

All of the interviews were collected in two waves from late December 2004 to late January 2005 and May 2005. I also conducted several pilot interviews with black teachers who taught outside the tri-county area. Initially, through community nomination, I derived a working list of 147 names of black teachers who are long-time residents of Edgecombe, Nash, and Wilson counties.[2] In the first wave of interviews, I used local telephone directories to locate individuals from my list of possible participants. Although there were more women than men on the list, it was difficult to find married women because their telephone numbers were usually listed under their husband's name. In the interviews, I sought participants' assistance in my efforts to locate "missing" women teachers who still lived in the area. Participants were able to offer such assistance because within a county, participants usually lived across the street, down the road, or around the corner from each other.[3] I asked every participant to identify additional teachers I should interview, which added only six names to my original list and gave me a total of 153 teachers who could potentially be interviewed. Due to time and funding constraints, I chose to interview every fifth person on the list and, in seven cases, I also conducted joint interviews with the spouses of participants who were teachers in the same school system. The total number of 44 participants included both individual and joint interviews from community nomination.

In a well-cited article, educational historian Jack Dougherty (1999) cautioned against an overuse of snowball sampling in historical and qualitative research on black schools and teachers.[4] Consequently, I adopted a strategy of "maximum variation" sampling to avoid a simple convenience sample (Patton, 1990; Strauss and Corbin, 1998). As Patton (1990) explained: "Any common patterns that emerge from variation are of particular interest and value in capturing core experiences and central shared aspects" (p. 172). Purposively and non-randomly, I selected my interviewees so that they included people from different social and political circles, intentionally seeking to create maximum variation. I deliberately asked informants to identify former teachers who might have a different experience from their own. For instance, I would ask a participant who taught at the high school level to recommend an elementary teacher.[5] Vanessa Siddle Walker (1996) also noted that she looked for variability in her study of the all-black school she attended in Caswell County, North Carolina: "I also sought interviewees who would have a range of relationships to the school, including students who completed high school as those who didn't, parents who lived varying distances from the school, and students who were involved in numerous school activities and those who were not" (p. 22).

Ultimately, I used what I had been told about people to determine which people I worked hardest to track down, with a self-conscious strategy of seeking to cover the full range of experiences. I talked to as many people as time and money would allow and ceased interviewing once I discovered that little new data (e.g., stories, topics, or people) were being presented (Strauss and Corbin, 1998). I sought to achieve as diverse a sample as possible being certain to include: teachers of different sexes; teachers who taught in primary (1–3), grammar (4–7 or 4–8), and high school (8–12); teachers who taught in county and "city" schools; teachers from different types of colleges, such as normal schools, teachers colleges, state universities, and small liberal arts colleges; teachers who were in different age cohorts—sixties, seventies, eighties, and nineties; teachers who left the classroom (quit or changed careers) and those who retired in education; and, finally, teachers who were married and those who had never been married. Merriam (1998) quoting Patton, has concluded that "findings from even 'a small sample of great diversity' yields 'important shared patterns that cut across cases and derive their significance from having emerged out of heterogeneity'" (p. 63). Maximum variation sampling required me to search for "disconfirming instances or variations" among my list of living participants (Merriam, 1998, p. 63). The total number of participants were chosen for maximum diversity of experiences.

Archival and Secondary Historical Data

To be sure, the accounts from these 44 teachers have been influenced by the days, months, and years since the 1954 *Brown* decision (Shircliffe, 2001, 2006; Hamlin, 2002). Schwartz and Schuman (2005) have suggested the use of survey research in collective memory studies as a traditional methodology that could, in my case, allow a comparison of what these teachers might have thought in earlier decades to what they believe now. Other than a published study of North Carolina black principals in the early 1970s by Frederick A. Rogers, which I use throughout the book, I have found no surveys in which black teachers were asked to give their opinions of black schools and education in the Age of Jim Crow.

Archival research confirmed and disconfirmed stories that participants told. I located archival data for my analysis from the archives of five historically black colleges and universities in North Carolina: Bennett College and North Carolina Agricultural and Technical State University in Greensboro, Fayetteville State University in Fayetteville and Saint Augustine's College and Shaw University in Raleigh. Fourteen participants attended Fayetteville State Teachers' College, one of three all-black "teachers colleges" in North Carolina during the Age of Jim Crow.[6] The other two teachers' colleges were Winston-Salem State Teachers' College and Elizabeth City State Teachers' College. Although I did not use all of the archival materials that I collected, my analysis has been shaped and reshaped from what I read and learned from institutional handbooks, photographs, college bulletins and school yearbooks.

In addition, the North Carolina Collection at the University of North Carolina at Chapel Hill proved to be most helpful to the study. The North Carolina Collection provided multiple volumes of newspaper clippings about "Afro-Americans Teachers" and "Afro-American Education," which I searched from the mid 1940s (when some participants began teacher preparation) to 1975 (when all schools had been desegregated or closed). This archival source holds over a quarter of a million printed items documenting the history and literature of North Carolina and its people. There are numerous editions of "State School Facts" that compare white, Indian, and Negro students, faculties, and buildings throughout the Jim Crow years.

Secondary historical materials complemented the archival data, which I used to layout a textually mediated memory of segregated schools for blacks (Wertsch, 2001). While some of the sources that I used construct a history of Southern black schools before integration as backwards and inferior (e.g. Frazier, 1957; Tyack and Cuban, 1995), others seek to reconstruct a collective memory and history of segregated schools as good and positive environments for the education of black youth—despite the lack of financial resources and white supremacy (e.g. Siddle Walker, 1996b; Foster, 1997). The secondary historical materials include literary historical fiction, historical analyses, and personal narratives. While individual and collective remembering is "always subject to the nostalgic interpretation of experience," as Beauboeuf-Lafontant (1999) explained, the "points of convergence in these separate investigations of black segregated schools are many and they suggest in a compelling manner that African Americans are recalling aspects of their history that warrant the attention of educational researchers" (p. 710).

Analysis

All interviews were transcribed and I used an analytic-inductive process to organize the data (Miles and Huberman, 1994; Strauss and Corbin, 1988). I read the data numerous times using a line-by-line analysis to identify themes and patterns (Strauss and Corbin, 1998). After common themes and patterns were identified, I coded and recoded the data looking for every instance in which a participant talked about a particular theme, such as "pedagogy," "class and other hierarchies," and "respectability." (I noticed early in the coding process that participants referred to the teaching profession as "respectable" work.) Furthermore, I clustered my data around codes in order to uncover multiple and contradictory experiences among participants. In accordance with maximum variation sampling (Patton, 1990; Strauss and Corbin, 1998), I became confident when I noticed that common patterns and central themes emerged that could be used to extend existing theory on how and why teachers taught in legally segregated schools for blacks.

My analytical approach in this multiple site study differs from single site studies, such as Siddle Walker (1996), in two important ways. First, I am able to explore multiple settings to enhance generalizability (Huberman & Miles, 1994). Although the purpose of this study is not to generalize about black teachers everywhere, maximum variation sampling enabled me to talk about participants' experiences across counties and across schools. Second, my research data points to thematic collective remembering across schools and communities, and thus helped to address valid criticisms that previous findings in one school or community are anecdotal and limited to a specific setting.

Appendix B

INTERVIEW QUESTIONS

Family and Educational Background

Full Name:
Year of Graduation from High School (age):
Parents' Occupations:
Schools attended (from elementary to college):
Number of years taught:
Teaching Career:

___ First Occupation ___ Second Occupation ___ Third Occupation

___ 1–3 Grades ___ 4–6 Grades ___ 6–8 Grades ___ 9–12 Subject

___ All-black schools only ___ All-black schools/Integrated Schools

Why did you decide to become a teacher?
Professional Memberships: (e.g., North Carolina Teachers Association and Sorority or Fraternity)

Teaching in Legally Segregated Schools for Blacks

1. What do you remember about teaching in the all-black school before integration?
2. How did you get your first teaching position? Tell me more about your first teaching position.
3. In the school(s) where you taught before integration, what do you remember about the quality of education children received?
4. What are your best and worst memories of teaching in the all-black school before integration?
5. What kinds of memorabilia (e.g., yearbooks, letters, teacher handbooks, pictures) have you kept of the years in which you worked in the all-black school?

6. Were you committed to school integration before the federal mandate to desegregate with "all deliberate speed?"
7. Reflecting upon our conversation and what you remember about the all-black school, what has been lost or gained because of school integration?
8. Scholars have dismissed some positive aspects of teaching and learning in segregated schools for blacks as "romanticizing the past?" What do you think?
9. What haven't we talked about that should be mentioned in a book about the all-black school?
10. Who should I talk to next?

Appendix C

Table Demographics and Characteristics of the Total Number of Participants

Participants	Sex	Age	Undergraduate	Graduate	Teaching Area
Beasley, Annie	F	76	Shaw	NCCU (M.A.)	English & French
Bobbit, Alton	M	74	ECSTC	ECU (M.Ed.)	Grades 6–8
Branford, Charles	M	81	WSTC	PSU (M.Ed.)	Grades 6–8
Branford, Susie	F	71	FSTC	N/A	Grades 1–3
Brown, Maureen	F	71	St. Augustine	N/A	Grades 4–6
Buchanan, James	M	67	NCA&T	ECU (M.Ed.)	Grades 6–8/ Principal
Burks, Gloria	F	71	St. Augustine	N/A	Music/Special Ed
Cameron, Amanda	F	79	FSTC	N/A	Grades 6–8
Cooper, Carol	F	59	St. Augustine	N/A	Grades 6–8
Coston, Fannie	F	73	FSTC	N/A	Grades 4–6
Cummings, Elmer	M	74	NCCU	IU/Duke (M.Ed./Ph.D.)	Grades 6–8/ Principal
Davis, Henry	M	76	NCA&T	N/A	Social Studies
Edwards, Josephine	F	83	FSTC	PSU (M.Ed.)	Grades 6–8
Edwards, Lucille	F	67	Shaw	N/A	Grades 6–8
Emory, Athalene	F	75	Bennett	N/A	French
Forbes, Thelma	F	67	FSTC	N/A	Grades 1–3
Foster, Julia	F	80	FSTC	NYU (M.Ed.)	Grades 1–3
Foster, Terrence	M	83	FSTC	Columbia (M.Ed.)	Grades 4–8/ Principal

Continued

Appendix C

Participants	Sex	Age	Undergraduate	Graduate	Teaching Area
Gray, Gloria	F	69	Bennett	N/A	Englich & French
Gray, Samuel	M	73	MSU	N/A	Physical Education & Science
Hines, Arcenia	F	85	ECSTC	N/A	Grades 1–5
Hines, Catherine	F	74	Spelman	ECU (M.Ed.)	Home Economics & Grades 1–3
Hines, Mildred	F	70	WSTC	U. Maryland (M.Ed.)	Grades 6–8
Hunter, Nellie	F	72	St. Augustine	N/A	Social Studies
Jones, Doretha	F	63	FSTC	N/A	Grades 1–3
Jones, Jessie	F	76	Shaw	PSU (M.S.)	Chemistry
Lewis, Cleveland	M	73	NCA&T	N/A	Biology
Lewis, Hazel	F	68	Shaw	N/A	Grades 1–3
Lucas, Equiller	F	62	FSTC	N/A	Grades 3–6
Odom, Mary	F	79	FSTC	N/A	Grades 1–3
Pitt, Roosevelt	M	69	NCA&T	NCA&T (M.Ed.)	Music/Pricipal
Pulley, Ada	F	74	WSTC	NCCU (M.Ed.)	Grades 4–6/ Special Education
Pulley, Herbert	M	74	NCA&T	NCA&T (M.Ed.)	Science/ Counselor
Ray, Joseph	M	75	NCCU	NCCU (M.Ed.)	Physical Education/ Principal
Ricks, Anniebelle	M	71	FSTC	N/A	Grades 4–6
Ricks, Joseph	M	65	St. Augustine	ASU (M.Ed.)	Speech
Smith, Effie	F	70	FSTC	N/A	Grades 1–5

Appendix C 113

Participants	Sex	Age	Undergraduate	Graduate	Teaching Area
Taylor, Catherine	F	73	JCSU	Duke (M.Ed.)	English
Toney, Helen	F	73	FSTC	N/A	Grades 1–3
Turner, Dianne	F	62	Bennett	NCCU (M.Ed.)	Social Studies/Counselor
Turner, William	M	64	NCCU	N/A	Biology
Tyson, Vera	F	76	WSTC	N/A	Grades 1–3
White, Pauline	F	75	WSTC	N/A	Grades 1–3/Kindergarten
Williams, James	M	60	NCA&T	NCA&T (M.Ed.)	Biology/Principal

List of Educational Institutions:

  Appalachian State University (ASU)
  Bennett College (Bennett)
  Columbia University (Columbia)
  Duke University (Duke)
  East Carolina University (ECU)
  Elizabeth City State Teachers College (ECSTC) (now Elizabeth City State University)
  Fayetteville State Teachers College (FSTC) (now Fayetteville State University)
  Indiana University (IU)
  Johnson C. Smith University (JCSU)
  Maryland State University (MSU) (now University of Maryland at Eastern Shore)
  New York University (NYU)
  North Carolina Agricultural and Technical State University (NCA&T)
  North Carolina Central University (NCCU)
  Pennsylvania State University (PSU)
  Shaw University (Shaw)
  Spelman College (Spelman)
  St. Augustine's College (St. Augustine)
  University of Maryland at College Park (UMaryland)
  Winston-Salem Teachers College (WSTC) (now Winston-Salem State University)

Notes

NOTES TO CHAPTER 1

1. The term, "Jim Crow," originated around 1830 when Thomas Rice—a white man in black face—mimicked black people as part of a performance entitled "Jump Jim Crow" (for a detailed discussion, see C. Vann Woodward's classic The Strange Career of Jim Crow). Over time, state sponsored legal segregation and discrimination began to be referred to as Jim Crow laws and practices, such as "quadruple public bathrooms, special trains and tramways, separate restaurants and hotels, double waiting rooms, [and] colored coded drinking fountains" (Lewis, 1993, p. 270).
2. For example, Adam Fairclough (2001) found that "much of the sociological evidence about black schools derives from the 1930s, and the strongest theme of Depression-era reports is how awful they were. Investigators compiled a grim picture of classes still being held in dilapidated buildings, leaning at impossible angles, that lacked adequate lighting, heating, toilets, washing facilities, and even basic items like desks and tables. In such places a solitary teacher, usually a young woman with little more than a high-school education, struggled with classes of as many as seventy-five children spread over eight grades" (p. 48).
3. James Wertsch (2002) defines a textual community as "a collective whose thought and action are grounded in written texts, but for at least some members this grounding may be indirect" (p. 28).
4. James Wertsch (2002) has noted that "one response to this line of reasoning might be that what [he] is proposing is not really a form of memory at all, but instead a type of knowledge—namely, knowledge of texts" (p. 27). Citing John Gardiner and Richardson-Klavehn (2000), Wertsch's (2002) work acknowledges that memory can be "an intensely personal experience of the past" and can involve situations "in which we are aware of knowledge that we possess but in a more impersonal way" (p. 27). Choosing to use the term "collective memory" instead of "collective knowledge" because it is more familiar, Wertsch maintains that "a coherent account of collective memory can be based on notions of knowledge of texts, a line of reasoning behind the notion of 'textual communities' (p. 27).

NOTES TO CHAPTER 3

1. Fortunately, Rodgers provides a detailed narrative about his methodology which I read thoroughly to determine the reliability and validity of his

results. After careful consideration, I decided that Rodgers study was a gem to be integrated within my text and a key secondary historical source on the social organization of the black public high school in North Carolina.
2. As Rodgers (1975) noted, "Most of the principals (40 percent) answering the questionnaire administered schools located in the eastern part of North Carolina. About 59 percent of these black high schools were in rural areas or in small towns of less than two thousand. The majority (60 percent) of the students in the black high schools represented came from rural areas" (p. 35).
3. Rodgers (1975) interviewed twenty black principals about "how they ran their schools, on what sorts of duties were required of them by law, and what they actually had to do. They were also queried as to the role they themselves and their schools played in community life" and twenty white superintendents "mainly with an eye to putting the role of the black high school and the black high school principal in the perspective of the larger community. [He was] particularly interested in finding out whether or not they were aware of the roles, other than that required by law, that the black principal chose to play or was forced to play" (p. 105),
4. According to Rodgers (1975), he sent letters to the superintendents of 151 school districts asking them to give the names of the all black high schools that had been operating in their districts in 1963-1964 and the last year the schools had functioned as an all-black high school. He derived a list of 177 formerly all-black high schools which he added 10 names from the 1963-64 Educational Directory of North Carolina. He sent out 187 questionnaires and received 58 completed questionnaires which he analyzed in the fall of 1973.
5. For more information about the displacement of black teachers in the transition from segregated to desegregated schools, see Michael Fultz's "The displacement of black educators post-Brown: An overview and analysis," James Haney's "The effects of the Brown decision on black educators" and Robert Hooker's *Displacement of the black teachers in the eleven southern states*. Full citations are provided in the bibliography.
6. The dominant narrative insists that black schools had poor teaching and unqualified teachers. It would be easy to dismiss what teachers told me in interviews or to attribute their accounts to false memories, nostalgia, or a collective attempt to claim virtues that they did not possess.
7. I use 1939-1940 North Carolina Department of Public Instruction (NCDPI) data because of the reference that Tyack and Cuban (1995) make about black teachers in 1940. None of the teachers that I interviewed had started teaching before 1940. According to the NCDPI, the index of training considered the number and percentage of teachers and principals in accordance with the number of years training in high school or college. Unless otherwise indicated, these data were derived from the NCDPI State School Facts for July 1941.
8. James Anderson (1988) concluded that "the development of teacher training programs for black students in the South evolved at a slower pace, in large part because southern white school authorities were unwilling to enforce equally high standards for black schools" (p. 113).
9. Rodgers (1975) argued that "as the country became involved in World War II, white teachers found more profitable jobs in areas other than teaching. This did not hold true for black teachers. As a result of this, white teachers left their profession in great numbers, and by 1948 there were sixty times more nonstandard certificate holders among white teachers than in 1937" (p. 32).

10. According to Rodgers (1975), "Salaries also reflected [the] difference in training, since the law passed in 1944 equalized salary schedules. Black teachers' salaries were 103 percent those of white teachers in 1950-51 as opposed to 73 percent of whites' salaries in 1940" (p. 32).
11. For a complete breakdown of participants, degrees earned, and subjects taught, see appendix C.
12. Unless otherwise indicated, these data have been taken from Rodgers (1975).

NOTES TO CHAPTER 4

1. Other scholars (Beauboeuf-Lafontant, 2002; Foster, 1991; Irvine & Hill, 1990) have explored how both race and gender politics shaped black teachers' lives and work.
2. In addition to Siddle Walker's work, the field of black teachers' work has benefited greatly from foundational historical studies written by Anderson (1988), Fairclough (2000, 2001, 2004, 2007), Fultz (1995), and Perkins (1983, 1989). For a more recent overview with suggestions for further research, see "'As Is the Teacher, So Is the School': Future Directions in the Historiography of African American Teachers," in William J. Reese and John L. Rury (eds.), Rethinking the History of American Education (New York: Palgrave MacMillan, 2008), 73-102.
3. Some of the teachers I interviewed mentioned that some children did agricultural work only during the summers and after school; some parents did not allow their work in the fields to interfere with their schooling.
4. Most teachers said that they had access to a "duplicating machine" that was usually kept in the office. Teachers had to copy texts onto a stencil and then make duplicate copies by manually turning a knob. Before this duplicating machine, teachers talked about using a "jelly substance" and a press to make copies.
5. Rodgers (1975) reported that "some of the students in the black high school felt that they had better communication with the teachers and more opportunity to participate in extracurricular activities" (p. 48).
6. In their interviews, teachers talked about why they decided to stay in teaching. Most of them acknowledged that there were few opportunities for college-educated blacks in North Carolina. Teaching was considered a respectable job that had a dependable wage.

NOTES TO CHAPTER 5

1. Other black professionals and organizations chose to focus, more or less, on acquiring cultural, social, or economic capital, such as the National Council of Negro Women, the National Negro Business League, and the National Association for the Advancement of Colored People. Teachers were members of many of these organizations, which afforded an intricate overlap in goals, objectives, and missions across organizations. There were a host of local religious denominations and mutual aid societies that participants in my study joined as dues-paying members during the Jim Crow years.
2. In an effort to think about the relationship between educational capital and cultural capital within black schools in the Age of Jim Crow, historian John

H. Bracey quoted the Roman philosopher, Terence: "Nothing human is alien to me." According to Bracey, the formal knowledge in all black schools was broad and without limits. The goal was to prepare black students to live in a world broader than the black world. (Personal interview, October 26, 2005)
3. By the mid 1940s to 1960s, when the teachers I interviewed started teaching, black teachers were certainly more likely to prepare black youth for future possibilities and opportunities than for Negro jobs and second-class citizenship (See Anderson, 1988).
4. In my interviews, several teachers mentioned "copying" materials for mass usage. I questioned teachers about the likelihood of there being a "copy machine" in their schools. Most teachers said that they had access to a "duplicating machine" that was usually kept in the office. Teachers had to copy texts onto a stencil and then make duplicate copies by manually turning a knob. Before this duplicating machine, teachers talked about using a "jelly substance" and a press to make copies.
5. This phrase was the actual class motto of the 1954 graduating class of Swift Creek School in Nash County, North Carolina. One of the participants, Hazel Williams Lewis, graduated from this school. A copy of the annual, the *Beaver*, is in the author's possession.
6. In their interviews, teachers talked about why they decided to stay in teaching. Most of them acknowledged that there were few opportunities for college-educated blacks in North Carolina. Teaching was considered a respectable job that had a dependable wage. There were two major reasons that participants gave for not leaving the teaching profession: family obligations and love of teaching.

NOTES TO THE APPENDIX

1. In appendix B, I have provided a complete list of interview questions.
2. Community nomination is a term coined by Michele Foster (1990, 1997) to legitimate securing informants through direct contact with the local community. I used community nomination to identify former teachers believed to be alive and living in the area.
3. I discovered from participants that this geographical arrangement has a historical basis. Due to racial segregation across the three counties I studied, black teachers could purchase homes only in black neighborhoods.
4. In his critique of snowball sampling, for example, Dougherty (1999) stated: "Unknowingly, we often narrow our analyses by interviewing participants within the same social and political circles as the first contact, thus excluding alternative perspectives. Of course, this approach may be necessary for oral history topics with few known witnesses or survivors or in pioneering fields of research where little has been written. But to advance the history of teachers' work, we might borrow methods from social scientists, such as stratified sampling or purposive sampling, to gather perspectives intentionally from members of different hierarchical levels or subgroups of the whole. While not random sampling, these approaches may help us to think more systematically about whose oral histories we choose to record and the claims we make while analyzing them" (p. 719–20).
5. I did not attempt to interview two former teachers who were identified as being "incoherent" or "not alert," as well as several teachers who were sick when I contacted them for an interview. Unfortunately, I was not able to interview a cohort of former teachers in these counties who were lured to

urban schools in the North by the National Educational Association just before school integration in North Carolina.
6. Fayetteville State University (originally State Normal School) was the first normal school for blacks in North Carolina. Until 1960, the only major the school offered was education. Source: Smith, Jessie Carney. (2003). *Black Firsts: 4,000 Ground-Breaking and Pioneering Historical Events*. Second Edition. Detroit, MI: Visible Ink Press.

Bibliography

Archival Materials

Chapel Hill, North Carolina
   University of North Carolina at Chapel Hill, North Carolina Collection, Louis Round Wilson Library
Fayetteville, North Carolina
   Fayetteville State University Special Collections and Archives, Charles W. Chesnutt Library
Greensboro, North Carolina
   Bennett College Special Collections and Archives, Thomas F. Holgate Library*
   North Carolina A&T State University Archives, Ferdinand D. Bluford Library*
Raleigh, North Carolina
   Saint Augustine's College Archives, Prezell R. Robinson Library*
   Shaw University Archives, James E. Cheek Library*

(*)Asterisk indicates that the author retrieved and analyzed documents from archive but did not cite materials within text.

Oral History Interviews

Beasley, Annie. December 29, 2004.
Bobbit, Alton. January 12, 2005.
Branford, Charles. January 4, 2005.
Branford, Susie. January 4, 2005.
Brown, Maureen. January 6, 2005.
Buchanan, James. January 8, 2005.
Burks, Gloria. May 20, 2005.
Cameron, Amanda. May 23, 2005.
Cooper, Carol. January 3, 2005.
Coston, Fannie. January 13, 2005.
Cummings, Elmer. May 24, 2005.
Davis, Henry. May 19, 2005.
Edwards, Josephine. December 21, 2004.
Edwards, Lucille. January 14, 2005.
Emory, Athalene. January 11, 2005.
Forbes, Thelma. May 18, 2005.

Foster, Julia. January 4, 2005.
Foster, Terrence "T.V.". January 4, 2005.
Gray, Gloria. May 18, 2005.
Gray, Samuel. May 18, 2005.
Hines, Arcenia. May 25, 2005.
Hines, Catherine. December 31, 2004.
Hines, Mildred. May 25, 2005.
Hunter, Nellie. May 23, 2005.
Jones, Doretha. January 14, 2005.
Jones, Jessie. May 19, 2005.
Lewis, Cleveland. December 22, 2004.
Lewis, Hazel. December 22, 2004.
Lucas, Equiller. May 20, 2005.
Odom, Mary. May 25, 2005.
Pitt, Roosevelt. May 16, 2005.
Pulley, Ada. January 7, 2005.
Pulley, Herbert. January 7, 2005.
Ray, Joseph. May 25, 2005.
Ray, Joseph. May 25, 2005.
Ricks, Anniebelle. December 28, 2004
Ricks, Joseph. December 28, 2004.
Smith, Effie. December 27, 2004.
Taylor, Catherine. January 11, 2005.
Toney, Helen. January 5, 2005.
Turner, Dianne. May 18, 2005.
Turner, William. May 18, 2005.
Tyson, Vera. May 25, 2005.
White, Pauline. January 6, 2005.
Williams, James. December 28, 2004.

Books and Articles

Anderson, E. (1990). *Streetwise: Race, class, and change in an urban community*. Chicago, IL: University of Chicago Press.

Anderson, J. (1988). *The education of blacks in the south, 1860–1935*. Chapel Hill, NC: University of North Carolina Press.

Assmann, J. (1995). Collective memory and cultural identity. *New German Critique*, 65, 125-133. Translated by J. Czaplicka.

Beauboeuf-Lafontant, T. (1999). A movement against and beyond boundaries: 'Politically relevant teaching' among African American teachers. *Teachers College Record*, 100(4), 702–723.

Beauboeuf-Lafontant, T. (2002). A womanist experience of caring: Understanding the pedagogy of exemplary black women teachers. *The Urban Review*, 34(1), 71–86.

Becker, G. (1993). *Human Capital*. 4th edition. Chicago, IL: University of Chicago Press.

Bennett deMarrais, K. & LeCompte, M. 1999. *The Way Schools Work: A Sociological Analysis of Education* (3rd ed.). New York: Longman.

Bond, H. (1934). *The education of the Negro in the American social order.* New York: Prentice-Hall.
Bourdieu, P. (1977). Cultural reproduction and social reproduction. In J. Karabel and A. Halsey. (Ed.), *Power and ideology in education.* (pp. 487–511). New York: Oxford University Press.
Bourdieu, P. (1984). *Distinction: A social critique of the judgement of taste.* (Richard Nice, Trans). Cambridge, MA: Harvard University Press.
Bourdieu, P. (1986). The forms of capital. In J. Richardon (Ed.), *Handbook of Theory and Research for the Sociology of Culture* (pp. 241–58). New York: Greenwood Press.
Brown, L. (2008). *Upbuilding Black Durham: Gender, class, and Black community development in the Jim Crow South.* Chapel Hill, NC: University of North Carolina Press.
Carter, P. (2003). "Black" cultural capital, status positioning, and schooling conflicts for low-income African American youth. *Social Problems,* 50(1), 136–155.
Carter, P. (2005). *Keepin' it real: School success beyond black and white.* New York: Oxford University Press.
Cecelski, D. (1994). *Along freedom road: Hyde County, North Carolina and the fate of black schools in the South.* Chapel Hill, NC: University of North Carolina Press.
Chafe, S., Gavins, R., & Korstad, R. (2001). *Remembering Jim Crow: African-Americans tell about life in the segregated South.* New York: The New Press.
Connerton, P. (1989). *How societies remember.* Cambridge: Cambridge University Press.
Coser, L. A. (1992). (Ed). *Maurice Halbwachs: On collective memory.* Chicago, IL: University of Chicago Press.
Cross, B. (2003). Learning or unlearning racism: Transferring teacher education curriculum to classroom practices. *Theory Into Practice,* 42(3), 203–209.
Delaney, D. (1998). *Race, place, and the law, 1836–1948.* Austin, TX: University of Texas Press.
Delpit, L. (1995). *Other people's children: Cultural conflict in the classroom.* NY: Free Press.
Dempsey, V. & Noblit, G. (1993). The demise of caring in an African American community: One consequence of school desegregation. *The Urban Review,* 25(1), 46–61.
DiMaggio, P. (1982). Cultural capital and school success: The impact of status culture participation of the grades of U.S. high school students. *American Sociological Review,* 47, 189–201.
Dixson, A. & Rousseau, C. (2006). *Critical Race Theory in Education: All God's Children Got a Song.* New York: Routledge Press.
Dougherty, J. (1998). 'That's when we were marching for jobs:' Black teachers and the early civil rights movement in Milwaukee. *History of Education Quarterly,* 38(2), 121–141.
Dougherty, J. (1999). From anecdote to analysis: Oral interviews and new scholarship in educational history. *Journal of American History,* 86(2), 712–723.
Du Bois, W. E. B. (1994). The coming of John. *The souls of black folk.* New York: Gramercy Books. (Original work published in 1903).
Du Bois, W. E. B. (2002). The training of Negroes for social power. In Provenzo, E. E. (Ed.). *Du Bois on education.* New York: AltaMira Press. (Original work published in 1903)
Errante, A. (2000). But sometimes you're not part of the story: Oral histories and ways of remembering and telling. *Educational Researcher,* 29(2), 16–27.
Fabre, G. & O'Meally, R. (1994). *History & memory in African-American culture.* New York: Oxford University Press.

Fairclough, A. (2000). 'Being in the field of education and also being a Negro . . . seems . . . tragic:' Black teachers in the Jim Crow South. *Journal of American History*, 87(1), 65–91.

Fairclough, A. (2001). *Teaching equality: Black schools in the Age of Jim Crow.* Athens, GA: University of Georgia Press.

Fairclough, A. (2004). The costs of *Brown*: Black teachers and school integration. *Journal of American History*, 91(1), 43–55.

Fairclough, A. (2007). *A class of their own: Black teachers in the segregated school.* Cambridge, MA: Harvard University Press.

Fentress, J. & Wickham, C. (1992). *Social Memory.* Oxford: Blackwell.

Foster, M. (1990). The politics of race: Through the eyes of African-American teachers. *Journal of Education*, 172(3), 123–141.

Foster, M. (1991). Constancy, connectedness, and constraints in the lives of African-American teachers. *NWSA Journal*, 3(2), 233–261.

Foster, M. (1993). Educating for competence in community and culture: Exploring the views of exemplary African-American teachers. *Urban Education*, 27(4), 370–394.

Foster, M. (1997). *Black teachers on teaching.* New York: New Press.

Frankenberg, E. and Lee, C. (2002). *Race in American public schools: Rapidly resegregating school districts.* Cambridge, MA: The Civil Rights Project, Harvard University.

Frankenberg, E., Lee, C., and Orfield, G. (2003). *A multiracial society with segregated schools: Are we losing the dream?* Cambridge, MA: The Civil Rights Project, Harvard University.

Franklin, J. H. (2005). *Mirror to America: The autobiography of John Hope Franklin.* New York: Farrar, Straus, & Giroux Publishers.

Franklin, J. H. & Moss, A. A. (1994). *From slavery to freedom: A history of African Americans* (7th ed.). New York: McGraw-Hill.

Franklin, J. L. (1994). Black southerners, shared experience, and place: A reflection. *The Journal of Southern History.* 60(1), 3–18.

Franklin, V. P. (1990). They rose and fell together: African-American educators and community leadership, 1795–1954." *Journal of Education*, 173(3), 39–64.

Franklin, V.P. & Savage, C. J. (2004). *Cultural capital and black education: African American communities and the funding of black schooling, 1865 to the present.* Greenwich, CT: Information Age Publishing.

Frazier, E. F. (1957). *Black Bourgeoisie.* Glencoe, IL: The Free Press.

Frederick Douglass Alumni Association Souvenir Journal. 1993. (August)

Fultz, M. (1995). Teacher training and African American education in the South, 1900-1940. *Journal of Negro Education*, 64(2), 196–210.

Fultz, M. (2004). The displacement of black educators post-*Brown*: An overview and analysis. *History of Education Quarterly*, 44(1), 11–45.

Fultz, M. (2008). 'As Is the Teacher, So Is the School': Future Directions in the Historiography of African American Teachers," in W. J. Reese and J. L. Rury (Eds.), *Rethinking the History of American Education* (pp. 73–102). New York: Palgrave MacMillan.

Gaillard, F. (1988). *The dream long deferred.* Chapel Hill, NC: The University of North Carolina Press.

Gaines, K. (1996). *Uplifting the race: Black leadership, politics, and culture in the twentieth century.* Chapel Hill, NC: University of North Carolina Press.

Gilmore, G. E. (1996). *Gender & Jim Crow: Women and the politics of white supremacy in North Carolina, 1896-1920.* Chapel Hill, NC: University of North Carolina Press.

Gould, M. (1999). Race and theory: Culture, poverty, and adaptation to discrimination in Wilson and Ogbu. *Sociological Theory*, 17(2), 171–200.

Hamlin, F. (2002). 'The book hasn't closed, the story is not finished:' Coahoma County, Mississippi, civil rights, and the recovery of a history." *Sound Historian*, 8, 37–60.
Hampton, H. (1986). *Eyes on the Prize*. [PBS video series]. Boston, MA: Blackside Production.
Haney, J. E. (1978). The effects of the *Brown* decision on black educators. *Journal of Negro Education*, 47, 88–95.
Higginbotham, E. B. (1993). *Righteous discontent: Women's movement in the black Baptist church, 1880–1920*. Cambridge, MA: Harvard University Press.
Holley, D. (2005). Is *Brown* dying? Exploring the resegregation trend in our public schools. *New York Law Review*, 49, 1085–1107.
Hooker, R. (1970). *Displacement of the black teachers in the eleven southern states*. Nashville, TN: Race Relations Information Center.
Huberman, A. M. & Miles, M. B. (1994). Data management and analysis methods. In N.K. Denzin & Y.S. Lincoln (Eds.), *Handbook of qualitative research* (pp. 428–444). Thousand Oaks, CA.: Sage.
Hundley, M. (1965). *The Dunbar story (1870-1955)*. New York: Vantage Press.
Irvine, J. (1989). Beyond role models: An examination of cultural influences on the pedagogical perspectives of black teachers. *Peabody Journal of Education*, 66(4), 51–63.
Irvine, J. (1990). *Black students and school failure*. Westport, CT: Greenwood Press.
Irvine, J. & Hill, L. (1990). From plantation to school house: The rise and decline of black women teachers. *Humanity & Society*, 14(3), 244–256.
Jeffries, R. (1994). The trickster figure in African-American teaching: pre- and postdesegregation. *The Urban Review*, 26(4), 289–304.
Jones, F. C. (1981). *A traditional model of educational excellence: Dunbar High school of Little Rock, Arkansas*. Washington, DC: Howard University Press.
Jones, S. (2006). Review of Race-ing Moral Formation: African American Perspectives on Care and Justice. *Educational Studies*, 39(3), 296–301.
King, J. and Ladson-Billings, G. (1990). The teacher education challenge in elite university settings: Developing critical perspectives for teaching in a democratic and multicultural society. *European Journal of Intercultural Studies*, 1, 15–30.
King, S. (1993). The limited presence of African-American teachers. *Review of Educational Research*, 63(2), 115–149.
Kingston, P.W. (2001). The unfulfilled promise of cultural capital theory." *Sociology of Education*, 74, 88–99.
Kozol, J. (2005). *The shame of the nation: The restoration of apartheid schooling in America*. New York: Crown Publishers.
Kruger-Kahloula, A. (1994). On the Wrong Side of the Fence: Racial Segregation in American Cemeteries. In G. Fabre and R. O'Meally. (Ed). *History & Memory in African-American Culture* (pp. 130–149). New York: Oxford University Press.
Ladson-Billings, G. (1995). Toward a theory of culturally relevant pedagogy. *American Educational Research Journal*, 32(3), 465–491.
Ladson-Billings, G. (2000). Fighting for our lives: Preparing teachers to teach African American students. *Journal of Teacher Education*, 51(3), 206–214.
Lamont, M. and Lareau, A. (1988). Cultural capital: Allusions, gaps and glissandos in recent theoretical developments. *Sociological Theory*, 6, 153–168.
Lareau, A. and Horvat, E. M. (1999). Moments of social inclusion and exclusion: Race, class, and cultural capital in family-school relationships. *Sociology of Education*, 72, 37–53.
Lather, P. & Ellsworth, E. (Eds). (1996a). Situated pedagogies: Classroom practices in postmodern times [Special issue]. *Theory into Practice*, 35, 2.
Lather, P. & Ellsworth, E. (Eds). (1996b). This issue. *Theory into Practice*, 35, 2, 70–71.

Lawrence-Lightfoot, S. (1995). *Balm in Gilead: Journey of a healer*. New York: Penguin Books. (Second Printing)
Leloudis, J. L. (1996). *Schooling the new South: Pedagogy, self, and society in North Carolina, 1980–1920*. Chapel Hill, NC: University of North Carolina Press.
Lewis, D. L. (1993). *W. E. B. Du Bois: Biography of a race, 1868–1919*. New York: Henry Holt.
Liberato, A., Fennell, D., & Jeffries, W. L. (2008). I still remember America: Senior African Americans talk about segregation. *Journal of African American Studies*. 12(3), 229–242.
Litwack, L. (1979). *Been in the storm so long: The aftermath of slavery*. Chapel Hill, NC: University of North Carolina Press.
Litwack, L. (1998). *Trouble in mind: Black southerners in the age of Jim Crow*. New York: Knopf.
McCullough-Garrett, A. (1993). Reclaiming the African American vision for teaching: Toward an educational conversation. *Journal of Negro Education*, 62(4), 433–440.
McHenry, E. (2002). *Forgotten readers: Recovering the lost history of African American literary societies*. Durham, NC: Duke University Press.
Martin, W. E. (1998). *Brown v. Board of Education: A brief history with documents*. Boston, MA: Bedford/St. Martin's Press.
May, V. (2007). *Anna Julia Cooper, visionary black feminist: A critical introduction*. New York: Routledge Press.
Merriam, S. B. (1998). *Qualitative research and case study applications in education*. San Francisco, CA: Jossey Boss Publishers.
Middleton, D. & Edwards, D. (1990). *Collective remembering*. London: Sage Publications.
Miles, M. B. & Huberman, A. M. (1994). *Qualitative data analysis: An expanded sourcebook*. Thousand Oaks, CA: Sage.
Mills, C. W. (1959). *The Sociological Imagination*. New York: Oxford University Press.
Morris, V. G. & Morris, C. L. (2002). *The price they paid: Desegregation in an African American community*. New York: Teachers College Press.
Mullane, D. (Ed.). (1993). *Crossing the danger water: Three hundred years of African-American writing*. New York: Double Day Publishing.
Murray, M. (2001). *Women becoming mathematicians*. Cambridge, MA: MIT Press.
Noblit, G. & Dempsey V. (1996). *The social construction of virtue: The moral life of schools*. Albany, NY: State University of New York Press.
North Carolina State School Facts. (July 1941). North Carolina State Department of Public Instruction, the North Carolina Collection at the University of North Carolina at Chapel Hill.
Ogbu, J. (1981). Origins of human competence: a cultural-ecological perspective. *Child Development*, 52(2), 413–429.
Ogbu, J. (1982). Cultural discontinuities and schooling. *Anthropology and Education Quarterly*, 13(4), 290–307.
Ogbu, J. (2003). *Black students in an affluent suburb: a study of academic disengagement*. Mahwah, NJ: Lawrence Erlbaum.
Olick, J. and Robbins, J. Social memory studies: From 'collective memory' to the historical sociology of mnemonic practices. *Annual Review of Sociology*, 24, 105–140.
Orfield, G. (2001). *Schools more separate: Consequences of a decade of resegregation*. Cambridge, MA: The Civil Rights Project, Harvard University.
Orfield, G. and Eaton, S. (Eds.). (1996). *Dismantling desegregation: The quiet reversal of Brown v. Board of Education*. New York: New Press.

Orfield, G. and Monfort, F. (1988). *Racial change and desegregation in large school districts: Trends through the 1986-87 school year.* Alexandria: National School Boards Association.

Packard, J. M. (2002). *American Nightmare: The History of Jim Crow.* New York: St. Martin's Press.

Patterson, J. T. (2001). *Brown v. Board of Education: A civil rights milestone and its troubled legacy.* New York: Oxford University Press.

Patton, M. Q. (1990). *Qualitative evaluation and research methods.* Second Edition. Newbury Park, CA: Sage Publications.

Perkins, L. (1983). The impact of the 'cult of true womanhood' on the education of black women. *Journal of Social Issues,* 39(3), 17–28.

Perkins, L. (1989). The history of Blacks in teaching. In D. Warren (Ed). *American teachers: History of a profession at work.* (pp. 344–367). New York: Macmillian.

Perry, T. (1975). *History of the American Teachers Association.* Washington, D.C.: National Education Association.

Philipsen, M. (1993). Values-spoken and values-lived: Female African Americans' educational experiences in rural North Carolina. *The Journal of Negro Education,* 62(4), 419–426.

Philipsen, M. (1999). *Values-spoken and values-lived: Race and the cultural consequences of a school closing.* Cresskill, NJ: Hampton Press.

Ramsey, S. (2008). *Reading, writing, and segregation: A century of black women teachers in Nashville.* Urbana-Champaign, IL: University of Illinois Press.

Randolph, A. W. (2004). The memories of an all-black northern urban school: Good memories of leadership, teachers, and the curriculum. *Urban Education,* 39(6), 596–620.

Rist, R. (1970). Student social class and teacher expectations: The self-fulfilling prophecy in ghetto education. *Harvard Educational Review,* 40(3), 411–451.

Ritterhouse, J. (2006). *Growing up Jim Crow: How black and white southern children learned race.* Chapel Hill, NC: University of North Carolina Press.

Rodgers, F. A. (1975). *The black high school and its community.* Lexington, MA: Lexington Books.

Schuman, H. and Scott, J. (1989). Generations and collective memory. *American Sociological Review,* 54, 359–381.

Schwartz, B. & Schuman, H. (2005). History, commemoration, and belief: Abraham Lincoln in American memory, 1945–2001. *American Sociological Review,* 70(April), 183-203.

Scott, D. (1997). *Contempt and pity: Social policy and the image of the damaged Black psyche, 1880-1996.* Chapel Hill, NC: UNC Press.

Scott, J. (1990). *Domination and the arts of resistance: Hidden transcripts.* New Haven, CT: Yale University Press.

Shaw, S. (1996). *What a woman ought to be and to do: Black professional women workers during the Jim Crow era.* Chicago: University of Chicago Press.

Shircliffe, B. (2001). We got the best of that world: A case for the study of nostalgia in the oral history of school segregation. *Oral History Review,* 28(2), 59–84.

Shircliffe, B. (2006). *The best of that world: Historically black high schools and the crisis of desegregation in a southern metropolis.* Creskill, NJ: Hampton Press.

Siddle Walker, V. (1996a). Interpersonal caring in the "good" segregated schooling of African American children: Evidence from the case of Caswell County Training School. *The Urban Review,* 25(19), 63–77.

Siddle Walker, V. (1996b). *Their highest potential: An African American school community in the segregated South.* Chapel Hill, NC: University of North Carolina Press.

Siddle Walker, V. (2000). Valued segregated schools for African American children in the South, 1935–1969: A review of common themes and characteristics. *Review of Educational Research,* 70(3), 253–285.

Siddle Walker, V. (2001). African American teaching in the South: 1940–1960. *American Educational Research Journal*, 38(4), 751–779.

Siddle Walker, V. (2005). Organized resistance and Black educators' quest for school equality, 1878–1938. *Teachers College Record*, 107(3), 355–388.

Siddle Walker, V. (2009). *Hello professor: A Black principal and professional leadership in the segregated south.* Chapel Hill, NC: University of North Carolina Press.

Smith, J. C. (2003). *Black Firsts: 4,000 Ground-Breaking and Pioneering Historical Events.* Canton, MI: Visible Ink Press.

Sokol, J. (2006). *There goes my everything: White southerners in the Age of Civil Rights, 1945–1975.* New York: Knopf.

Sowell, T. (1976). Patterns of black excellence. *Public Interest*, 43, 26–58.

Strauss, A. & Corbin, J. (1998). *Basics of qualitative research: Techniques and procedures for developing grounded theory (2nd ed.).* Thousand Oaks, CA: Sage.

Taylor, E, Gillborn, D. & Ladson-Billings, J. (Eds.) (2009). *Foundations of Critical Race Theory in Education.* New York: Routledge Press.

Tickamyer, A. R. (2000). Space matters! Spatial inequality in future sociology. *Contemporary Sociology*, 29(6), 805–813.

Turner, R. (1986). Sponsored and contest mobility and the school system. In Arum R. and I. R. Beattie. *The Structure of schooling: Readings in the Sociology of Education.* (pp. 22–34). Boston, MA: McGraw-Hill.

Tyack, D. & Cuban, L. (1995). *Tinkering toward utopia: A century of public school reform.* Cambridge, MA: Harvard University Press.

Valentine, C. A. (1968). *Culture and poverty: Critique and counterproposals.* Chicago: University of Chicago Press.

Villegas, A. (1988). School failure and cultural mismatch: Another view. *The Urban Review*, 20, 253–265.

Watkins, W. (2001). *The white architects of black education: Ideology and power in America, 1865–1954.* New York: Teachers College Press.

Wertsch, J. (2001). Narratives as cultural tools in sociocultural analysis: Official history in Soviet and post-Soviet Russia. *Ethos*, 28(4), 511–533.

Wertsch, J. (2002). *Voices of collective remembering.* New York: Cambridge University Press.

White, M. (2004). Paradise lost: Teachers' perspectives on the use of cultural capital in the segregated schools of New Orleans, Louisiana. In Franklin, V.P. and C.J. Savage. *Cultural capital and black education: African American communities and the funding of Black schooling, 1865 to the present* (pp. 143–158). Greenwich, CT: Information Age Publishing.

Williams, J. (1998). *Thurgood Marshall: American Revolutionary.* New York: Three Rivers Press.

Wolcott, V. (1997). 'Bible, bath, and broom': Nannie Helen Burroughs, the National Training School, and the uplift of the race. *Journal of Women's History*, 9, 88–110.

Wolcott, V. (2001). *Remaking respectability: African American women in interwar Detroit.* Chapel Hill, NC: University of North Carolina Press.

Woodward, C. V. (1974). *The strange career of Jim Crow.* 3rd Rev. Ed. New York: Oxford University Press. (Original work published in 1955)

Wright, R. (1937/2001). The ethics of living Jim Crow: An autobiographical sketch. In P. S. Rothenberg. *Race, class, and gender in the United States: An integrated study.* 5th Ed. (pp. 21–30). New York: Worth Publishers.

Yosso, T. (2006). *Critical race counterstories along the Chicana/Chicano educational pipeline.* New York: Routledge Press.

Index

1895 Atlanta Exposition Address. *See* Booker T. Washington

A
Academic achievement
  Cultural deficits, 66
  Cultural mismatch, 66
  In legally segregated schools for blacks, 68
Agricultural economy. *See* Seasonal agricultural work
Alumni Association. *See* Frederick Douglass School Alumni Association
Anderson, Elijah, 21
Anderson, James, 28
Assmann, Jan, 6

B
Bad schools. *See* Inferior all-black schools
Balm in Gilead, 31. *See also* Sara Lawrence-Lightfoot
Barnes, Ed, 84
Beasley, Annie, 60–61, 74
"Bible, Bath, and Broom". *See* Nannie Helen Burroughs
Black Bourgeoisie. See also E. Franklin Frazier
Black child labor
  Reasons for, 28, 49
  Teachers' responses to, 29, 50
Black cultural knowledge. *See* Culturally relevant teaching
Black High School and its Community, The, 25, 30–31, 34, 35, 77, 79
Black middle class professionals
  Jobs of, 3, 14, 35, 38–39, 55
  Teachers as, 15, 39, 44–45

Black principals
  Dealing with white superintendents, 35, 76–77
  Expectations of, 35–36, 82
  Experiences of, 27, 35, 76, 84
  Involvement with parents and community, 35
  Nature of work, 76
  Power of, 77
  Relationships with teachers, 52, 77, 84
Black teachers
  And consequences, 26
  And creativity, 73, 74
  And loss of jobs, 26
  And three principles of respectability, 49
  As helpers, 51
  As resources, 53, 54
  As role models, 55, 59, 68
  Before federal desegregation, 25, 32, 43, 46
  "Bourgeois", 43–44, 59
  Certification of, 33
  Class tension between, 43, 62
  Description of, 3, 44
  Discipline by, 56, 60, 83–84
  Exemplary examples of, 33, 46–47
  Financial contributions, 53, 54
  Messages to students, 53, 58
  Motivation for actions, 4, 8, 24, 30
  On reasons for teaching, 36
  Overqualified, 33
  Politics of respectability, 15, 44, 97
  Principals' expectations of
  Teaching strategies, 66, 68, 71
  Training of, 32, 34
  Work of, 3, 18–19, 53, 54
Bobbitt, Alton, 33, 53–54, 84

Bourdieu, Pierre, 22. *See also* Capital
Branford, Susie, 28
Brown v. Board of Education, Topeka, Kansas
  1954 *Brown* decision, 7, 13
  1955 *Brown* decision, 7, 43
Brown, Leslie, 65
Brown, Maureen, 30
Buchanan, James, 53, 55–56
Burks, Gloria, 31, 62, 81, 84
Burroughs, Nannie Helen, 45

C

Capital
  As currency, 22–23
  As cultural capital, 22–23, 67, 69–71
  As economic capital, 22–23, 67, 71
  As human capital, 68
  As social capital, 22–23, 67, 71
  Educational. *See* Educational capital
  Forms of: embodied, objectified, institutionalized, 22–23, 67
Cameron, Amanda Mitchell, 76, 82–83, 87–88
Caring. *See* Good all-black schools
Celelski, David, 19, 26
Central High School, 7
Charlotte-Mecklenburg School System, 6
Child labor. *See* Black child labor
Civil Rights, 14, 46, 71, 97
Civil War, 85
Classrooms
  Grouping, 50–51
  Nature of, 13, 16, 36, 47, 50, 56, 58, 71–76, 78
  Role of teachers in, 54
Collective memory
  And the present, 5–7, 11–13
  And counter memory, 44, 47, 85
  Conflict in, 5, 35
  Definition of, 5
  Key points of, 5–6
  Negative collective memory, 4, 7, 43
  Multivoiced collective memory, 6
  Positive collective memory, 4, 10, 11, 13
  State production (official) of, 9
  Vicarious memory, 5
Collective remembering
  In terms of social and geopolitical context, 17
  And hidden transcripts, 24, 27
  Production of counter-memories, 51
  Wertsch's theory of, 6
Commemorations, 4
Community nomination, 104
Connerton, Paul, 4
Constant comparative method, 48
Cooper, Anna Julia, 45
Cooper, Carol, 57
Coston, Fannie, 50, 74
Counts, Dorothy. 7
Counter-hegemonic acts and struggles, 97
Cuban, Larry. *See* David Tyack and Larry Cuban
Cultural capital
  And educational capital, 67
Cultural knowledge. *See* Culturally relevant teaching
Culturally relevant teaching, 47, 50
Cultural signals (high and low), 22, 67, 69
Cummings, E.J., 56, 80, 85
Curriculum and instruction
  And educational capital, 67
  And situated pedagogies, 66, 68, 71
  Extracurricular activities, 49
  Human resources, 67, 81
  Religion in, 79

D

Darden High School (Charles H. Darden High School), 50, 62
Davis, Henry, 56–57, 84, 87
Delaney, David, 17–19
Double-consciousness
  And educational capital, 67, 100–101
  Definition of, 86
  Racial pride, 87, 88
Dougherty, Jack, 104
Dream Long Deferred, The, 6
Du Bois, W.E.B., 37, 45, 70, 86
Durham Morning Herald, 35

E

Edgecombe County (North Carolina), 18, 25–26, 28, 34, 48, 73, 97, 103–104
Educated fool, 37
Educational capital
  And human capital, 68
  And racial knowledge, 70, 79
  Basic principles of, 67–68
  Consequences of, 70
  Conversion of, 71
  Definition of, 67

In Jim Crow schools, 54, 68
Limitations of, 96
Pierre Bourdieu's definition of, 67
Edwards, Josephine, 16, 29, 49, 52, 54, 58, 62, 74, 78, 85
Edwards, Lucille, 29, 56
Elm City High School (Also known as Frederick Douglass School), 33, 53
Emory, Athalene, 30, 5, 61, 63, 73, 75, 78, 83–84
Errante, Antoinette, 5
Eyes on the Prize, 43

F
Fayetteville State Teachers College, 73
Flexible grouping. See Classrooms
Forbes, Thelma, 74
Foster, Julia, 79
Foster, Michele, 26, 43, 47–49, 63, 72
Foster, T.V., 76, 79
Franklin, John Hope, 70
Frazier, E. Franklin, 14, 43, 47
Frederick Douglass School Alumni Association, 3. See also Elm City High School
Fugett, Mr. (White superintendent), 76

G
Gaillard, Frye, 6–7
Gaines, Kevin, 45, 56
Geopolitics of race and racism
    Along with geographies of power, 21
    Definition of, 17
    In preparing black youth for skilled jobs, civil rights and social power, 54, 97
Gilmore, Glenda, 45
Good all-black schools
    And violent interactions, 31
    Caring in, 54, 55, 57
    Exemplary, 33, 45, 61
"Good English", 78
Good neighbors, 100
Granville, Evelyn Boyd, 59
Gray, Gloria, 29, 32
Gray, Samuel, 57–58, 76
Great Depression, 46, 64

H
Halbwach, Maurice, 5
Hamlin, 24
Harding High School, 7
Hidden transcripts

As power, 56, 93
And collective remembering, 17, 24, 93, 98
Definition of, 4, 13, 24
Delicacy of, 27
Public records confirming, 35, 93
Higginbotham, Evelyn Brooks, 45
Hines, Arcenia, 36–37, 51–52
Hines, Catherine, 52, 75
Hines, Mildred, 31, 74
"Hometown girls" or "hometown boys", 39
Human resources, 67, 81
Hunter, Nellie, 55–56, 58–59, 62, 78, 80, 83, 86

I
Industrial education. See Booker T. Washington
"Inferior" all-black schools, 13, 32
Internalized racism, 56

J
Jim Crow South
    Practices of, 19
    Racial Segregation, 23
    Racial Etiquette, 21–22, 37
    Social meanings of, 19, 32
Jim Crow's teachers. See Black teachers
Jim Crow wisdom, 20–22, 94
Johnson, Mr. (black principal), 76
Johnson, Robert A., 3
Jones, Doretha, 56, 58, 60
Jones, Jessie, 60–61, 74
Jones, Sylvia, 63

K
Kozol, Jonathan, 100–101

L
Ladson-Billings, Gloria, 50, 66, 101
Lawrence-Lightfoot, Sara, 31
Leloudis, James, 16
Lewis, Cleveland, 52, 74, 84
Lewis, David Levering, 86
Lewis, Hazel, 36–37, 52, 75
Lincoln School, 76
Litwack, Leon, 85
Lucas, Equiller, 28, 52

M
Marshall, Thurgood, 13
Materials and supplies
    And educational capital, 67

And lessons, 80
Intangible resources as, 73
Resource deprivation, 17
Tangible resources as, 73, 76, 81
Teachers' contributions, 54
Maximum variation sampling, 105, 107

N
Nash Central Training School for Negroes, 16
Nash County (North Carolina), 16, 18, 25–26, 28, 48, 62, 73, 97, 103–104
National Association for the Advancement of Colored People (NAACP), 74
National Education Association (NEA), 26
Nice, Richard, 23, 67
Nondominant cultural capital, 69. See also Capital
North Carolina Civil Rights Advisory Committee, 35
North Carolina Department of Public Instruction (NCDPI), 25, 34
Nostalgia, 11–12, 17, 48

O
Odom, Mary, 74
"Of the Coming of John", 37
Oral history
  As text, 9,
  As a methodology, 12, 18, 67
  Interview data, 103–104

P
Pitt, Roosevelt, 29, 37, 58
Pope, O.R., 84
Principals. See Black principals and White schools
Public school reform, 32
Pulley, Ada, 75, 83, 87
Pulley, Herbert, 80

R
Racial etiquette, 21–22, 37. See also Jim Crow South
Racial twoness, 86. See also Double Consciousness
Racial uplift
  Definition of, 22,
  Consequences of, 45, 55, 63
  Task of, 69, 87
Randolph, Adah Ward, 14, 77

Ray, Joseph, 60
Reader's Digest, 74
Resegregation of public schools, 99–100
Respectability
  Bourgeois, 44–46, 56
  Culture of, 69, 106
  Definition of, 14
  Politics of, 15. 44, 46, 97. See also Black teachers
  Promotion of, 86
  Morals and Manners, 53, 70
  Three teaching principles of, 49
Ricks, Anniebelle, 52, 80, 87
Roberts, Gus, 7
Rodgers, Frederick A. *See The Black High School and its Community*

S
Scott, James, 23
Seasonal agricultural work
  And different locations, 28
  Consequences of, 28, 49
  Responses to, 29
Separate but equal laws, 72
Shaw University, 36
Shircliffe, Barbara, 11, 14
Siddle Walker, Vanessa, 9, 14, 35, 43–44, 47–49, 54, 57, 63, 77–78, 107
Situated pedagogies, 66, 68, 71
Smith, Effie, 54–55, 73
Special education, 80
Social meanings of Jim Crow, 17–18, 24
Sociology of education, 66
Souls of Black Folks. See "Of the Coming of John"
South. See Jim Crow South
Sowell, Thomas, 13
Southern agricultural economy. See seasonal agricultural work
Street wisdom, 20. See also Jim Crow wisdom
State-mandated curricula, 68
Study methodology
  Archival Research, 105–106
  Collective Memory, 5
  Oral history interviews, 67, 103–104
  Participant selection, 104
  Secondary Sources, 105–106

T
Talented Tenth. See W.E.B. Du Bois
"Task Force Survey of Displacement in Seventeen Southern States"

Limitations of, 27
Taylor, Catherine, 49, 50, 54, 75, 77–78
Teachers. *See* Black teachers
Teacher positioning, 35, 77
Teacher tax, 52
Teaching
  As a calling, 82–83, 95–96
  As a geopolitical practice, 50
  As a profession, 53
  In rural schools, 73, 77
  Team teaching, 49
Textbooks, 8, 9, 13, 32, 50, 53, 73, 76, 80
Textual community, 7, 9
Their Highest Potential, 48
Toney, Ben, 81
Toney, Helen, 38, 50, 52, 78, 79
Turner, Dianne, 36–37, 76, 80, 85
Turner, Ralph, 57
Tyack, David and Larry Cuban, 32, 34
Tyson, Vera, 60, 84

U
University of North Carolina at Chapel Hill, 34, 106
Uplift ideology. *See* Racial uplift

W
Washington, Booker T.
  And industrial education, 45, 70
  And the 1895 Atlanta Exposition address, 70
Wertsch, James, 5, 23
White, Monica, 55
White, Pauline, 38, 51–52, 64
Whiteness
  Psychological presence of, 30, 32
White principals. *See* White schools
White schools
  And white principals, 31
  Coon High and Fike High as, 30
  Relationship with, 30, 76
Winston-Salem State Teachers College, 38
Wilson County (North Carolina), 3, 18, 25–26, 28, 30, 48, 80, 97
Wolcott, Victoria, 46
World War II, 46
Wright, Richard
  And social meaning, 17, 18, 94
  Capital in the Jim Crow South, 23. *See also* Capital
  Respect, 22
  Visions of uplift, 22

For Product Safety Concerns and Information please contact our EU representative GPSR@taylorandfrancis.com
Taylor & Francis Verlag GmbH, Kaufingerstraße 24, 80331 München, Germany

www.ingramcontent.com/pod-product-compliance
Lightning Source LLC
Chambersburg PA
CBHW052051300426
44117CB00012B/2069